LEE MILT

Author of *Success Is*

SPIRITUAL
POWER TOOLS

FOR SUCCESSFUL SELLING

Harnessing the Power of Your Mind with

Intuition, Vision, and Self-discipline

"I started reading *Spiritual Power Tools for Successful Selling* the minute it arrived, and I didn't stop until I finished! Norman Vincent Peale once admonished his audience to 'find a need and fill it.' While we often think of such advice in terms of volunteerism, Lee Milteer has skillfully demonstrated that spiritual principles are winning principles in the business world as well. If you're in sales, this isn't just a book to read—it's a book you should use—every day!"

—Barbara Hemphill, author, *Kiplinger's Taming the Paper Tiger at Work*

"*Spiritual Power Tools*, Lee Milteer beautifully melds two concepts . . . POWER and SPIRITUAL as shares her 'secrets' and practical ideas that she has applied to the world of successful selling. This thorough guidebook offers a 'higher plane' process we can follow in our lives."

—Susan RoAne, business speaker and best-selling author *How To Work a Room* and *How To Create Your Own Luck*

"*Spiritual Power Tools* is a book about ethics, and the new model of selling. You will learn from Lee Milteer about creating relationships, not just making deals. This will give you the tools for honoring your customers by being sensitive to their needs, interests and desires.

"Sales managers will find this ground breaking information and useful for their sales meetings to inspire their staff."

—Patricia Fripp, CSP, CPAE, Past President National Speakers Association, author *Get What You Want*

"Lee Milteer reveals in this book the true secrets for achieving success that have endured the test of time. She brilliantly translates abstract and complex topics into simple to use tools in plain down to earth language. It is a must read for anyone who wants to achieve and accomplish more in their careers while feeling a deep sense of profound grace and ease. I highly recommend this book if you want to be in integrity with yourself and be very prosperous."

—Dr. Ernesto J. Fernandez, DOM, LMHC

Also by Lee Milteer

Success Is an Inside Job

SPIRITUAL POWER TOOLS

FOR SUCCESSFUL SELLING

LEE MILTEER

HAMPTON ROADS
PUBLISHING COMPANY, INC.

Cover design by Tiffany McCord
Cover digital imagery copyright © Getty Images/PictureQuest. All rights reserved.
Hampton Roads Publishing Company, Inc.
1125 Stoney Ridge Road
Charlottesville, VA 22902

434-296-2772
fax: 434-296-5096
e-mail: hrpc@hrpub.com
www.hrpub.com

If you are unable to order this book from your local
bookseller, you may order directly from the publisher.
Call 1-800-766-8009, toll-free.

Library of Congress Cataloging-in-Publication Data

Milteer, Lee.
Spiritual power tools for successful selling / Lee Milteer.
    p. cm.
Summary: "Advice from a motivational speaker and former saleswoman about
interjecting your spiritual beliefs into your everyday worklife in order to both
improve your productivity and heighten your enjoyment on the job"—Provided by
publisher.
Includes bibliographical references.
ISBN 1-57174-428-2 (5-1/2x8-1/2 : alk. paper)
1. Selling. 2. Business ethics. 3. Business—Religious aspects. I.
Title.
HF5438.25.M58 2005
248.8'8—dc22
2005019780

ISBN 1-57174-428-2

10 9 8 7 6 5 4 3 2 1

Printed on acid-free paper in the United States

To Angel

Contents

Acknowledgments

This book is truly the result of a team effort. I extend my deepest gratitude and appreciation to:

Robert Friedman, my publisher from Hampton Roads Publishing, for believing in me and encouraging me to write, first, *Success Is an Inside Job,* and now this book, *Spiritual Power Tools for Successful Selling.* I am so grateful for your vision and your belief in me.

Clifton D. Williams, Jr., my other half, for your love, support, and understanding during what has been one of the greatest professional challenges of my life—writing this book. Thanks for understanding the long hours, the sacrificed evenings and weekends. Clif, you are the wind beneath my wings. I truly appreciate your unceasing love, support, and encouragement.

Pamela Brothers Denyes, the editor of my manuscript. Your eagle eye and attention to detail are awesome. Thank you for your deep insights and your ability to boil down my long production of written words into a manageable manuscript. Thank you for helping me stay on course and for putting the materials in a workable order. Thanks for the long hours and spiritual support.

Donna Reed Corbet, my office manager, for your incredible support running my office while I was writing. Your ability to manage and coordinate my coaching programs and speaking engagements, as well as your enthusiastic encouragement, is truly appreciated.

Dan Kennedy for being my friend and one of the greatest support systems I could ask for. Dan, your marketing and business genius has assisted me more than words can say. I will always be in awe of your wisdom and friendship.

To my Millionaire Mindset sponsors, clients, coaching members, and friends who have shared their dreams, struggles, and triumphs with me. It gave me the courage to speak my truth. I appreciate your perseverance in the face of adversity and the amazing lives you have all created. You were the inspiration that led me to write this book and share these tools.

And, most of all, I want to thank God for assisting me to move past all fears, doubt, and insecurity of "who am I to write a book called *Spiritual Power Tools*." Thank you, God, for touching my life with vision, purpose, and passion.

Introduction

Anyone who has picked up this book is interested in more than just making commissions and winning sales contests. You want to incorporate universal spiritual principles into your daily work life that will empower you to be prosperous and successful and serve the needs of your clientele.

My intention is to share with you some ways of thinking about what you do that you can use to develop new habits of thought and actions that you can take to improve your sales skill and boost sales results. Even more important, learning and using these spiritual tools will contribute to your sense of well-being and joy in the sales process as well as in the service you render to your clients.

We live in a new world that is shifting toward a new level of consciousness. Money and success are still very important to us, but we also desire to live our lives with integrity, to achieve peace of mind, and to feel that life has deep meaning. We want our work to be rewarding and satisfying, not just profitable. We long to integrate our spiritual selves with our business practices.

Most people have been programmed to be afraid of the sales process and of salespeople. Can you imagine life without salespeople? Can you imagine how much time, energy, and expense it would take if we had to research the products and services we use all by ourselves? How drastically different life would be without salespeople to educate and assist us in obtaining the necessities of life! In fact, the entire structure of our society would be very different. You can be proud of the fact that you are helping people get what they want and need. Selling is one of the most important professions in the world.

There are always two or more parties to every sale: the salesperson and the person who makes the decision to buy. When salespeople learn to honor themselves, their contributions, and their own integrity, they automatically honor their customers. When you can honor yourself and honor your prospects, you can then focus on their needs, which will improve your ability to be of service, raise your self-esteem, and improve your closing rate.

In the world we live in today, I do not believe that just knowing how to sell is enough anymore. We must learn to see life—and our customers—from an entirely new perspective. Value has replaced image, and intrinsic worth has replaced name brands. Our clients are asking themselves very important questions, such as: *Does this feel real? What is quality? What is good service? Whom can I count on and believe in?* The old standard beliefs we hold about ourselves and about the world of sales must change.

Today's consumers are intelligent, alert, highly selective, and independent in their thinking. To work with today's consumers you must strive for excellence, integrity, and high ethics. You must also be someone who stands out from the competition.

Faith Popcorn, a leading-edge marketer and trend forecaster, whom *Fortune* magazine called "the Nostradamus of Marketing," writes in her best-selling book *The Popcorn Report* that "The Good Guy is back! Our whole idea of heroics is changing. We're going beyond knighting the richest, the cutest, the most powerful, and the sexiest. We are also saluting the Ethical Man who makes it his business—both literally and figuratively—to make the world a better place."

That's exactly what *Spiritual Power Tools for Successful Selling* is about: making life as a salesperson easier and more rewarding in all areas—physically, mentally, emotionally, spiritually, and financially.

In this new model of selling I focus on sales as a means of creating relationships, not just making deals. Together we'll explore tools for honoring customers, being sensitive to their needs, interests, and desires, and caring about what is right for them.

Spiritual selling means selling only what you believe in, what you have passion for, and what you can be completely honest about. When you add spirituality to "selling" you invite your God source to join you, and when you do that you tap into an unlimited wellspring of creativity, energy, love, and abundance.

William Brooks, author of *Niche Selling: How to Find Your Customer in a Crowded Market,* says, "Most traditional sales philosophies are outdated in today's crowded marketplace. The future belongs to the salespeople and organizations that are flexible and nontraditional in their thinking."

Last time I looked on Amazon.com there were hundreds of books on sales. Reading sales technique books can help you develop a system to follow while perfecting your trade and prevents you from having to reinvent the wheel. Many writers, such as Dan Kennedy, Brian Tracy, and Tom Hopkins, have already written extensively on the many aspects of technique selling. If you truly wish to be a great salesperson, I highly suggest that you invest time in reading from these many masters of sales and use their sales strategies techniques.

In this book, I focus on sharing with you ways to incorporate spiritual tools that will add balance and integrity to your work, increase your sales, improve your relationships with clients and customers, and improve your personal satisfaction as a sales professional. By adding such a spiritual dimension to your professional sales toolbox, you can improve your ability to be of service to others as well as increase your own enjoyment of the process of sales.

As a salesperson, I am sure you have noticed that as the world has changed, time seems to have speeded up. People seem to have less time and patience for anything that does not serve their immediate wants and needs. To be a successful salesperson today you must utilize every resource available to you. Every salesperson has a toolbox of skills, knowledge, and experience to draw from in his life and work. But the average salesperson doesn't think about the spiritual aspect of sales and focuses only on the standard techniques of selling. I suggest that by adding spiritual tools to your daily life you will find that you have an advantage over other salespeople.

I would like to state up front that adding a spiritual dimension to your sales techniques does not mean that you will sell every client or that you won't face the normal challenges of doing daily business. However, adding specific spiritual exercises to your toolbox will help you feel better about yourself and create a foundation of habits that can lead you to enjoy a greater success than you ever could have imagined.

Open yourself to a new level of thinking. Put aside your old opinions and the belief systems that have guided your sales career up to today. Read this information with an open mind and open heart. I am going to tell you the truth, as I know it, about how to move yourself from being an average salesperson to being a conscious salesperson.

The knowledge that I will share comes from my own years of sales experience, and from those I consider to be spiritual advisors and master salespeople. I will also share what I have learned through my extensive research into the underlying philosophies of proven success principles and spiritual teachings. And, of course, I'll share how these principles relate to the sales world that lies ahead of you.

A Personal Note

I want to share with you some personal background on my life and what led me to combine the sales profession with spirituality. By sharing some of my journey, I hope you will know that you are not alone in the obstacles and adversity you face. We all have our own journeys.

In no way do I feel that I have all the answers to everything. I always see myself as a lifetime learner and a student of universal knowledge. I hope that by reading my story, you, too, will give yourself permission to enhance your spiritual nature, to achieve peace of mind and fulfillment in your life's work, and to find the integrity to truly be yourself.

Since my earliest childhood I have always had a burning desire to understand and find my purpose in life. I can now look back and see that my entire life has been devoted to my search for truth and my soul's purpose. I was raised on a farm in rural Virginia that was one mile from the nearest secondary road and 18 miles from the nearest major grocery store. It was the house where my father was born, which was then more than 130 years old. When I look back now, I can see the many ways my life on the farm set the tone for the person I am today. I received a strong foundation in farm values, and the farm work ethic, and I developed a real connection to nature.

As a child I would wait until everyone had gone to bed at night; then

I would sneak outside and stare up at the vast expanse of starlight and wonder about life, and what I was supposed to do with mine. I felt like something was out there, something that felt good and safe and comforting, but I didn't know what it was.

My ancestors were farmers from as far back as we can trace. Because we were living on a farm and in touch with nature daily, my parents seemed more spiritual than religious, although we did attend Sunday school and church on Sunday and my brother and I went to Bible school every summer.

Even though my life on the farm was a good one, I just knew there had to be more to life than the cornfields. And so, when I was 17, I went to work at a local radio station as a disc jockey. Soon after I started, the sales manager asked if I would like to try working in sales. He spent several days telling me all about radio and how it helped people advertise. He explained what the new job could mean for me—independence and more money. It sounded very exciting. What he didn't tell me was that the station was rated last in the market and you couldn't give the advertising away! But what you don't know can't hurt you, so I hit the ground running. On my first day in the field I made a sale. On the second day I made two sales. My manager couldn't believe it. He was overwhelmed and so was I. He immediately doubled my salary and formally installed me in the sales department.

By the time I was 22 I had moved on to become sales manager for Background Music Service of Tidewater in Norfolk, Virginia. Within a short time this small company with only a few accounts was selling phone systems, intercoms, paging systems, and music to shopping centers, airports, and office buildings all over the region. And I had a reputation in sales as a hotshot.

Even in my early days in sales, I had a very customer-oriented approach, very rooted in service. I believed in responding to my customers' wants and needs and it worked very well. I began teaching my techniques to our sales staff—novice salespeople—and they became very high-volume earners.

My husband and I bought the service company where I sold electronic sound system equipment to commercial buildings; being self-employed gave us the means and the time to travel around the world for long periods of time as photographers, our passion and hobby at that time. Being a photographer and traveling around the world was one of the greatest educations of my life. Experiencing different cultures and becoming acquainted with various belief systems and traditions allowed me to appreciate and honor life from different perspectives. I developed a deeper sense of awareness of a more spiritual part of myself.

A major turning point in my life happened just two days before Christmas. It was an event that would change my life forever. I lost my beloved to a random and senseless violent crime. My world came crashing down on me in a way that I never could have dreamed possible. I felt I had hit an intense emotional bottom. Deeply disillusioned and depressed, I had days when I believed that I couldn't go on living. I began to question everything. How could this happen to me? What had I done to deserve such anguish? Is God really there? All of us, at some time in our lives, seem to pass through this period of darkness and loss of hope. The mystics call it the dark night of the soul. I called it "being in hell" at the time.

This very difficult loss forced me into a time of serious soul searching. Life challenged me to go within and ask myself who I was, why I was here, and what I was doing with my life. I took classes and seminars on self-improvement. I learned to meditate and found that it opened up a whole new world—an inner world that was quite unfamiliar. As I became more aware of the spiritual part of myself, I began to recognize that the physical world was not the ultimate reality. Deeply wanting to feel connected to something larger than myself, I started to read about many different religions. I revisited Christianity and went on to study Eastern philosophy, Judaism, and Native American Indian traditions. I was impressed with different aspects of each belief system.

I read books like *The Nature of Personal Reality* by Jane Roberts, *The Handbook to Higher Consciousness* by Ken Keyes, and *The Science of Mind* by Ernest Holmes. These books introduced me to the concept that I had an inner consciousness that could help me to create my own reality. This new awareness did not fit my former rational understanding of life and purpose.

The more I learned, and the more I explored this new idea of creating my own reality, the more I came to believe in a higher intelligence, a pure positive energy from the universe, a creative and loving force that is the source and substance of all reality. I realized that the true creative power I was feeling within me was coming from some source other than me. We call this God, Love, Christ Consciousness, Cosmic Intelligence, Higher Power, the Pure Positive Universal Energy, Spirit, Higher Self, I Am, the Force, Source, Inner Guidance, and many other names. It became my passion to learn how to create a deeper connection with this Source in my own life.

Looking back, I can see clearly how this very difficult time forced me out of my comfort zone and into a time of serious soul searching. As the Bible says, "Ask and you will receive." I did not feel I had a choice. My safety net was gone and now I had to start to fly solo. Circumstances were challenging me and forcing me to go within and question everything about my life, my beliefs, and my values. What did I, Lee Milteer, want to do with my life? I had to find the truth and break away from the social programming and cultural demands forced upon me from my earliest recollections. I had to break away from what society said was possible and find out what my God-Source knew was possible for me—my life purpose.

I was discovering that my cultural programming and upbringing had led me to believe that life was something that would *happen* to me and all I could do was make the best of it. I realized that society programs us to believe that we are victims of circumstances. Our society gives power to external events and people and not to the natural source of power within each of us. I was uncovering the truth that the power to create my destiny and all of life's details rested within me. I could *choose* to create my life and be the captain of my own ship, so to speak. This new view of life felt empowering and rewarding, and it brought me to a place where I was beginning to feel connected to a higher power for the first time.

As a business owner, I had always been goal driven. Now, for the first time, I was setting goals but surrendering the outcomes to the universe. The old saying "Let go and let God" was working for me. The more I relaxed into this new awareness, the more my life began to make sense.

I started having intuitive flashes of insight and awareness that were highly accurate and clearly coming from a source wiser than myself. I started listening to my intuition.

My personality or ego could never have known what I was coming to understand. I soon found that when my inner guidance told me something and I followed it, things worked out fine. When my logical, culturally programmed mind would step in and stop me from following my inner guidance, things did not turn out well. I was always sorry when I did not listen to that inner guidance.

That inner guidance led me to start my own business as a trainer and public speaker. As a speaker and author you are simply selling ideas and concepts. This is truly my calling in life. And as confusing as it had been in the past, it was now crystal clear what I was supposed to be doing with my life: I was to help others see their own potential and assist them with the techniques for finding a uniquely individual purpose.

After a number of years as a human potential speaker and author I began to notice that although the salespeople in my seminars were always searching for new ways to succeed in their work, they now seemed to want more than just new techniques. They wanted their work to be rewarding. They wanted to have a sense of pride about their profession and to feel like they were making a contribution. These desires are spiritual in nature and it takes spiritual techniques to bring about the new results they craved.

At the same time I began to feel the burnout of constant traveling and speaking. I was losing the passion for my work. This troubled me deeply since I believed it was my soul's purpose to share information with people, which would allow them to tap into their own potential and talents.

I went to one of my own spiritual teachers for a counseling session. She listened to me describe my dismay at not feeling connected to my career or happy with my life. Then this teacher I think of as an Earth Angel said something that changed my life forever. She said, "You are a deeply spiritual woman and you have devoted over 20 of your life to understanding universal spiritual truths. I have noticed that you live by day as a businesswoman in the mainstream world. You have created success in your field as well as being well respected. In your private life you seem to be more interested in spiritual growth. I think part of your disillusionment with your career at this point is that your life is divided into two parts. Maybe it's time you merged. Marry your true spiritual passion with your profession. This is where you will find true happiness. Establish a new integrity between your personal and professional self."

After this meeting, I felt as if a huge weight had been lifted off me. I could give myself permission to express my spiritual beliefs in my professional life. I don't have to convince anyone to do anything. What I have to do is live from a set of beliefs that honors who I am.

Believing that my external world is a reflection of my internal world, I realized that I simply wanted to live from the truth as I know it. No more masks. What you see is what you get. And I am not perfect in any way. Merging these spiritual tools into my professional life affirms and enhances my integrity with myself and validates my feeling of being one with something bigger than myself.

So, as you read these words, please understand that sharing these materials has been a huge leap of faith for me. At one time, I was afraid to say the word God on stage. I had seen other business speakers talk about their religious beliefs and I knew this sometimes turned people off in the business environment. My clients would often write on my pre-program speakers' questionnaires that speakers should avoid speaking about religion. Early in my career I had made a decision that I had to keep my spiritual beliefs and teachings separate from my business principles. Obviously I have abandoned this thinking, and I now believe I must share these universal spiritual truths because these are truly the reason behind my success in business.

But let's be clear: I am not talking about religion here. I am sharing with you simple tools that will allow you to honor your own spirituality. These tools can help you use your inner power to fortify the sales techniques and resources you are already applying in your life.

You have the power through God to create a joyful, happy, balanced, and prosperous sales career. You have the opportunity to use your professional life as a salesperson to make a difference in the world. Choose to use this book as a guide to help you create your own formula for success. Mold and shape this material to fit your own style and your own personality. Life is an adventure and your point of power to create is this very moment! Enjoy!

Power Tool Number 1—The Power of Respect for Yourself and Your Profession

No matter what our title or profession, anyone who has succeeded at anything is an effective salesperson. We are selling our talents and abilities, our experience, our point of view, our beliefs, our values, and our enthusiasm daily, in hundreds of different ways. For example: Teachers sell the benefits of learning and the usefulness of knowledge. Scientists sell their ideas to raise money for research. We sell our children the benefits of education, of being a productive and moral citizen. We sell our ideas when we speak or write. We sell our experience and potential in job interviews. We sell our point of view in a conversation or a negotiation process. We even sell our personalities (just the good traits) when we are in social situations or dating. We sell our time (life energy) when we go to work. No matter what we do in life, we are always selling in one form or another. Sales skills are necessary survival skills in the real world and clearly we are all in sales, whether we know it or not.

I have met many sales professionals who have lost their enthusiasm about being a salesperson. After talking with these people it's clear that the negative portrayal of the sales profession has affected them. It is up to each one of us to reverse the negative perception of the sales process and the way society views salespeople, one person and one sale at a time. We can do that by revamping the way we perceive ourselves and, then, our interactions with others.

There is an old saying: "The soul is awakened through service." In Marianne Williamson's book *A Return to Love*, she says in a chapter about work:

> You're in business to spread love. No matter what we do, we can make it our ministry. No matter what form our job or activity takes, the content is the same as everyone else's: We are here to minister to human hearts. If we talk to anyone, or see anyone, or even think of anyone, then we have the opportunity to bring more love into the universe. From a waitress to the head of a movie studio, from an elevator operator to the president of a nation, there is no one whose job is unimportant to God.

When we are willing to go beyond where we have been before and see a larger picture of our lives and our purpose, we can see that our presence and assistance have enhanced and helped many people. There are people who look up to us for guidance. We are their role models and we may not even know it.

Think back in your life to a time when someone told you something good about yourself or noticed that you had a talent or skill, and because that person inspired you, it changed your life. I call these people Earth Angels. They are around us all the time but, if you are not in a receptive state of mind, you might miss all the positive and uplifting things people say to you.

Just for fun, do this experiment: Keep track of all the positive comments you get in a day. Pay attention to the world around you giving you positive feedback. The more you notice, the more you will get.

Every Christmas, I enjoy watching the famous old movie *It's a Wonderful Life,* with Jimmy Stewart. It reminds me that I have contributed to and assisted others in many ways. We need to remind ourselves that the simple act of doing our job well and making someone else's life easier can make a difference.

In the last few years I have realized that most of the people in my training seminars want more than sales training. They may even get positive feedback about their sales skills, but they seem to want to find new ways to feel fulfilled and happy in their careers. Just earning a paycheck and keeping the boss happy doesn't fulfill the needs of their souls. They want to be proud of their work and their contributions. They want to feel their work has value and importance to others and they want to make the world a better place for themselves and their children.

The bottom line is that you will never be *really* good at sales unless you view your profession as deserving respect and honor. As salespeople we contribute to the well-being of others, and it's time we acknowledge the importance of being in sales and allow ourselves to appreciate our contributions. Daily, as salespeople, we are contributing our life energy, our knowledge, our products and services to the well-being of other human beings and companies.

Sales Attitude Adjustment Time

Did you know that according to opinion polls more than half of the people in North America dislike huge parts of their jobs? According to Nancy Anderson, author of *Work with Passion*, "People are demanding satisfaction—and meaning—from their work." And it's a well-established fact that you'll be much more productive if you love what you're doing. As Abraham Lincoln said, "Most people are about as happy as they make up their minds to be."

So let's think about it. What ultimately separates us from our work is our own attitudes: the commonly held notions that work is a drag or that the client is the problem. Let go of those ideas and you may discover the sales world itself isn't the problem. The first real way to make changes in the sales process is to look inside at how we think about our sales position. It's in your attitude. Success in life is 80 percent attitude and 20 percent aptitude.

In her book *Do What You Love, the Money Will Follow*, Marsha Sinetar says, "Most of us resist our jobs, and that benefits no one." We all have chores and responsibilities we don't like. "The antidote," she says, "is to *choose* to be whatever I am doing now." After all, if it's worth doing, it's worth doing well. So if you're making cold calls, do it with enthusiasm and clear intentions. "You can choose to do your work responsibly and consciously, and that means willingly putting our full focus into the task we're engaged in," Sinetar sums up.

Taking Action

One of the best ways to begin seeing yourself as more than a salesperson is to begin seeing yourself as an independent consultant, one who analyzes the data available and recommends certain products or services to your clients, based on their needs. This is the sales model of the future.

Just look at how the Internet has changed our reality. Example: My travel agent says that anyone who can get on the Internet can now browse throughout many vacation websites and see and hear the selling points of various resorts. The information available on the Internet has changed the way she deals with her clients. Now she sees herself as more a consultant than a salesperson. This new attitude has made her workday less stressful and more fun. She realized that when she stopped trying to sell and simply focused on serving her clients' needs, her business doubled at a time when many travel agencies were going out of business.

There are some very positive effects to changing your attitudes about sales and the work you do:

- You'll have more energy.
- You'll take more risks.
- You'll feel more positive and live in the moment.
- You'll find a sense of participation and ownership in creating.
- Your productivity will increase.
- Your prosperity will increase because you have created value to yourself and to others.

If you are an average person, there will be times in your life when you don't feel very enthusiastic about your current position. Maybe stress or disappointment has dampened your perspective. Keep in mind these words from George Bernard Shaw: "The people who get on in this world are the people who get up and look for the circumstances they want, and, if they cannot find them, make them."

You always get what you focus on; if you spend your time thinking about what you don't like about your work, on an unconscious level you are programming yourself not only to fail but to be unhappy. Think back to the beginning of your career. Remember all the excitement you felt getting into sales. Recommit your mental energy to getting back to that state of mind. This technique is called "choosing what you have already chosen." Recall and recapture that early zeal and you will find yourself in a state of mind that is resourceful and ready for success. All you have to do is simply count your blessings, then seek and acknowledge what is good about your daily work.

Make a list of all the reasons you enjoy your work. Write down what you're grateful for in your current sales position. List all the benefits of what you do now, what you are learning, and how you assist others. To remind you of these work blessings, make copies of your "Grateful for My Work List" and put them in places where you'll see them often. Add to your list as you find more things for which you are grateful. Remember, what you focus on expands in your life. Focus on the good to attract more good.

You must let go of self-judgment which implies that what you do and who you are are not important. You affect people daily with your attitudes, actions, and intentions. Yes, your thoughts as well as your actions affect people. Make a new life choice to understand your work life as an opportunity to partner with God.

This book is based on the simple idea that salespeople who are responsive to their customer's needs, interests, and desires are offering a very valuable and important service to mankind, their clients, and themselves. The old model of sales is commission-driven. We were taught to do whatever it takes, say whatever we have to say, in order to make the sale.

In this new model we view the sales profession from a spiritual perspective. We use our natural power of partnering with God by adding a dimension that will not only empower us but add value and meaning to the lives of all the people we encounter.

We must first and foremost treat others as we would wish to be treated. That means that we must always see our clients or customers as being connected to us. Our number one goal is to be looking after their well-being and give them the best we can offer. We must honor our fellow human beings and know that our life energy, products, or services are helping our clients. We are building relationships and trust, not just making sales.

As we all know, money and titles are wonderful things, but what we all search for most is the feeling that our life has meaning and purpose. We want to believe and feel that we have made a difference! We can experience meaning, purpose, and worldly advantages, if we are willing to let our God consciousness guide us daily. Our actions, thoughts, and behaviors must be rooted in a desire for the well-being of everyone.

I would like to end this chapter by sharing with you a prayer that I have been using for some time and that I believe will benefit anyone who uses it. I believe that prayer helps you to get clear about what you want to create in your life and then focuses your life energy to go in that direction. Use this prayer as a kick-start to writing your own prayers that address your own aspirations. Writing your own prayers adds a massive amount of power to writing your own life's script.

Prayer of the Conscious Salesperson

Dear God,

Please give me the insight and perception to rise above the mundane and use my talents, experience, and abilities to share love into the world with my actions and thoughts. Give my life a sense of purpose and joy. Use me as an instrument of light for you in the world with every soul I encounter. I surrender my job to you. Assist me to remember that my real job is to be of service and to send positive energy into the world.

Thank you, Amen.

Power Tool Number 2—The Power of Partnering with God

If we are going to adopt a new model of selling, we need to rely on something other than the old sales approaches based on theory and mind games. We need to understand how to use our mental, physical, emotional, and spiritual life energies more effectively. Integrating spiritual principles into the sales process adds a new dimension to your business life. Consciously partnering with your highest nature—with your God Source—allows you to let go of those old approaches and to replace them with effective, integrative techniques.

When we allow ourselves to become spiritual partners with God within our business, we move into greater maturity, service, and peace of mind, and, potentially, massive prosperity. As we evolve spiritually to new levels of understanding, compassion, and intuition, we can truly become experts in our field.

As I said earlier, I have made a commitment to make my spiritual-self and business-self lifetime partners. I am excited about this direction and find that I always have something new to learn. Allowing myself to explore the inner parts of my nature keeps me curious and open-minded about life.

I have been inspired by many books. One that stands out as helping

7

me to develop my spiritual awareness is M. Scott Peck's *The Road Less Traveled: A New Psychology of Love, Traditional Values, and Spiritual Growth.* He says, "Spiritually evolved people, by virtue of their discipline, mastery and love, are people of extraordinary competence, and in their competence they are called on to serve the world, and in their love they answer the call. They are inevitably, therefore, people of great power, although the world may generally behold them as quiet ordinary people, since more often than not they will exercise their power in quiet or even hidden ways."

We must start seeing our profession as one that is blessed by God. We can be ambassadors of goodwill and knowledge. We must know in our hearts that when we put our partnership with God first in our business, everything else will fall into place. The peace of mind this practice provides will improve every aspect of our lives and those around us. When we feel good about ourselves, we can be a provider of goodwill to all.

One person can make a difference if he decides to make a clear commitment to seeing himself as being of service and not just a salesperson. This more expansive view of our work helps us see life from a different perspective. We don't have to divide our lives into many separate areas. We can combine our spiritual code of beliefs and our work. We can see our life's work as our ministry, not just a job or a career. We have the power and ability, through our sales careers, to uplift and help other people to get what they want and need. By focusing on achieving a balanced, spiritually integrated sales career, we can literally bring in all the ready-to-buy customers we can serve!

Embrace a Spiritual Mindset

There are many writers more qualified than I to teach true spirituality. My credential is that I have been able to marry spiritual practices with business know-how and become very successful and financially secure. My job in sharing this material is to broaden your mind to new possibilities for accomplishment in your field of sales through the application of spiritual concepts. I also want to show you that you can be in total integrity with yourself and your sales work.

As I was writing this book I was asked, "Exactly what does it mean to have a spiritual mindset?" Let me state up front that I am not implying any particular religious orientation, nor am I being judgmental. No one is right or wrong. You have the free will and right to choose to believe whatever feels right to you personally. In order to help you connect your spirituality with your work, I am sharing the ideas in this book directly from my observations and my experiences.

Spiritually awake people have a conscious awareness of both the physical and the invisible dimensions. Spiritual people accept that there is more of life to understand than what they can comprehend with their five physical senses. They know that they are souls with bodies and that their souls are not defined by birth and death on Earth. They know that their souls are not controlled by the rules that govern the physical world. Spiritual people see life from a multidimensional perspective.

Spiritual people tend to be focused on their internal power and personal growth. They understand that they have the ability to decide how to interact with the physical world and how to frame their experiences with their minds. Powerful examples of the power of a centered, calm mind are found in the philosophies of aikido and other oriental martial arts. The core of these practices is to become at one with an external confronting energy to neutralize the threat rather than exerting an external force over the opponent.

Spiritual people are comfortable with the concept of inner guidance. They believe that there is an invisible, eternal part of themselves that is available for assistance whenever they need it. Spiritual people have an understanding that somehow they are all connected to each other. They look for the presence of God in each person they meet. Spiritual people know that their thoughts and prayers are co-creating their reality with God. They are motivated to align their efforts with their highest purpose in order to live life authentically.

Spiritual people value quiet time to listen for answers from their own God Source. Listening to spiritual guidance and intuition is valued more than programmed knowledge from the outside world.

Spiritual people behave as if the God Source in all life matters; they have a sense of responsibility to the world around them. Spiritual people believe in the teaching of forgiveness and the Golden Rule.

As spiritual salespeople—or conscious salespeople—we must become deliberate co-creators. Some rules suggested by many of the spiritual masters can help you create a life that is filled with prosperity, happy relationships, success, and vitality. These rules are known as universal laws, from which all reality is created.

One of the secrets of success is to learn to feel. We become successful by thinking right thoughts and feeling in the state of mind as if we are already where we want to be. Working, doing, striving, and sweating are not avenues to becoming more successful in the sales world. We create our life by the way we feel, not by trying to control external reality.

Physicists now agree that everything in life, whether it's a person, a chair, or a flower, vibrates because it is all pure energy. Everything we have in our lives at this minute in time we co-created by generating an energy wave (good or bad) into the energy field we call our reality. And since the most elemental law of physics states that like attracts like, the feeling behind the energy waves we generate attracts to us those things or circumstances which match our feelings.

Our thoughts, powered by strong emotions, create electromagnetic wave patterns of energy, which flow out from us and produce effects on other wave patterns. In other words, you could think of yourself as a living magnet. As hard as it may be to believe, you have been sending out intense emotional messages into the electron universe, which have been returned to you with the same emotional intensity. All the successes—you brought those to yourself. I'm sure you can also think of a negative situation where you may have been feeling angry, resentful, or frustrated, and you attracted a negative response. Had you been in a more neutral state of mind and emotion, your outcome would have been different.

I know your mind is racing around trying to disprove this information. You may not want to admit to yourself that when you are in an unresourceful state of mind, if you are angry or frustrated, more disagreements, upsets, arguments, or even accidents happen to and around you.

This principle is called the *law* of attraction for a reason. It's always true.

Picture this: There is magnetic energy attached to our thoughts, and all our thoughts are propelled by our emotions. Since we are magnetic energy generators, whatever magnetic energy we send out into the world (our vibrations) is exactly the same type that we attract back into our energy field. Think of it this way— if everything is vibrating waves, we, with our emotion-charged thoughts, attract to ourselves whatever or whoever is operating at the same frequency or wavelength and with the same type of energy.

For example, if you, as a salesperson, attended a chamber of commerce meeting with a truly confident, professional attitude, and in a relaxed state of mind, you would attract to yourself customers who would appreciate your confidence and demeanor, and they would be more open to purchasing your products. You would also tend to attract other people like yourself—salespeople! You are putting out a high magnetic frequency characterized by gratitude, laughter, joy, and happiness.

Let's say another sales professional attended the same meeting, but this person was frustrated, feeling jealous of others' success or honors, and just generally critical of others., I can tell you what that person will attract—people who are even angrier at the world than she is. That is called a vibrational match in the law of attraction. Low frequencies of fear, jealousy, anger, or powerlessness have the power to attract exactly the same energy as do higher frequencies.

Here is the big news! We are the initiators of the energy frequencies (low or high) that pretty reliably attract back to us what we send out. Many spiritual teachers have written that we are the creators of our own reality. We literally create our life experience through our thoughts. Every thought we have has some creative power. Furthermore, the deeper the personal emotion that is present at the time that we send forth our thoughts, the more quickly we will attract our results.

Our goal in becoming conscious salespeople is to acknowledge our personal power to use our life energy in effective and rewarding ways. In his book *The Seven Spiritual Laws of Success*, Deepak Chopra says, "The physical universe is nothing other than the Self curving back within Itself to experience Itself as spirit, mind, and physical matter. In other words, all processes of creation are processes through which the Self or divinity expresses Itself...The source of all creation is divinity (or the spirit)... and the object of creation is the physical universe (which includes the physical body). These three components of reality—spirit, mind, and body, or observer, the process of observing, and the observed—are essentially the same thing. They all come from the same place: the field of pure potentiality which is purely unmanifest." Dr. Chopra says that once you understand the physical laws of the universe and apply them in your life, anything you want can be created from these three components of reality—spirit, mind, and body.

I enjoyed *Excuse Me, Your Life Is Waiting*, by Lynn Grabhorn, who called her spiritual journey "the physics of thought." She says:

> As we embark on this adventure of living the law of attraction, we come very soon to the rather disturbing conclusion that there truly is no such thing as a victim, and that continuing to play the game of being a victim to anything or anybody guarantees only continued discontent from the relentless emission of low vibrations.
>
> Oh sure, the rest of the world is still doing it, blaming "them" for what happened rather than their feelings: blaming "circumstances" for their bad luck rather than their feelings, blaming the drunk on the freeway, or the rotten boss, or the economy, or God for messing them up, rather than their feelings.
>
> We may have been taught, and therefore have believed, that we live at the mercy of others, or fate, or luck, or chance; certainly that is what most people on this planet live by. But once you start to see the law of attraction in operation, you ultimately come to understand that there is no such thing as a victim: never has been, never will be. There is no good luck, bad luck, good fortune, or coincidence. There is no destiny, fate, or providence. There is no big judge in the sky keeping score on how right or wrong you're been. There is no Karma from past lives, no penance. That's all victim stuff. And there is not a victim among us, only co-creators in thought and feeling, powerful magnets attracting like bees to honey the matching frequency of our ever-flowing vibrations.

You never again have to believe that circumstances outside of you control your life. You never again have to believe that it is wrong to want. You never again have to believe that some great power outside yourself is pulling the strings, or that anyone or anything other than you is in control. You never again have to be afraid of "them" or "it," no matter who or what they may be, unless you so choose.

This knowledge provided me with an advantage over the average salesperson. I could be a great salesperson not only because I actually enjoy the entire process, but because I use this almost-secret weapon— the power to image my life and affect the outcomes of my reality.

When I understood and used the principles of the law of attraction, my life went from struggle to less struggle. If I focused on lack and fear-based emotions, my business would be nonexistent or barely there. But if I focused on giving exceptional service and making great sales, I did. And when I started prospering, I prospered more. My emotions were the personal thermostat for my success in life.

Once you become aware of universal laws and you actually use them in a conscious manner, you will never feel like a victim again. Actually, as a student of the power of the mind, you are part of a new breed of spiritual pioneers, beginning to break free of the media's mass victim-consciousness programming and from our collective mind patterns that have brought us much lack, pain, and unnecessary suffering. In fact, our God Source created us to thrive, prosper, have fun, learn, create, and accept ourselves as the co-creators that we are!

Create a New Perception of Your World

No matter where you are and what you are doing at this time, you can make your work your calling. You can make a daily choice that what you are doing right now is your opportunity to partner with God and to serve other human beings. Every person you interact with is your opportunity to share love and light on Earth.

A few years ago I watched a Barbara Walters interview with a famous movie star who was in New York City shooting a movie. In the interview this movie star talked about how we should not let other people color our life experiences with their negative attitudes. He went on to say that the producer who had hired him for this job had told him that he just hated New York because New Yorkers were the most difficult, rude people he had ever encountered. The movie star, whose faith is Buddhism, decided that, before he got to New York, he would try an experiment. During the first three days after he arrived in New York, for every person with whom he interacted or whom he simply saw, he would issue a silent prayer. He prayed for their health, happiness, and prosperity, for them and their families. The star went on to say that this experiment had been one of the best things he had ever done. Within four days he reported that he had never experienced people who were nicer or more cooperative than the people he met in New York City!

This interview had a profound effect on me. I started to experiment as to whether this concept could work for me. I began by simply blessing people as I walked through crowded malls or airports. As I stood in line for service, I focused my thoughts on blessing and sending love to the people around me. I am happy to report that this new experiment has improved my life significantly. People seem to go out of their way to give me excellent service.

Then I began to send out love and blessings to my business appointments before we met in person. I found that people were more receptive, more agreeable, and clearly nicer. Now I use this technique before I speak to any group and I am thoroughly convinced that it works. I have seen a marked difference in responses between the days I have used positive mental thoughts and the days I have not used them. I consider blessing the people I pass in the world to be one of my good habits. I know I am sending out positive "vibes," building a big spiritual bank account balance with the positive actions and thoughts I send into the world!

I operate from the "What you sow is what you reap" mindset. Since I am a self-fulfilling prophecy, simply depositing positive energy into my environment assures me that I will receive that positive energy back in various aspects of my life. The only way you can truly believe in and operate your life with this information is to actually give it a try. Start small and just try it for 30 days. I can say with great enthusiasm that you will get a more positive reaction from people to whom you have sent your blessing.

This new commitment to send positive, uplifting thoughts can make a huge difference not only in your sales figures, but also in the quality of the interactions you have with others. Please consider that your life's work is more than just showing up and doing your job. Keep in mind that everything you do, say, and think has an effect, not only on yourself but on those around you. Sending out positive thoughts literally can change the way you see and experience life. The people around you who will benefit from these positive messages may never know what you have been doing for them, but on an unconscious level they are picking up your thoughts and feelings and reacting to them.

As a speaker and author I am a salesperson of ideas. When I stand on stage and present information, I am aware of the fact that there are many things competing for the audience's attention. Not everyone in all audiences wants to be in a training session. Some people are compelled to attend at their bosses' direction. Some people may have had an unpleasant experience on their way to the session, such as getting lost or getting a speeding ticket. Numerous things can distract audience members and put them in a negative frame of mind before they even arrive at a presentation. We can all relate to these different distractions as they happen in our own lives.

Before I start to speak (to sell ideas) I focus on sending energy and love to the audience. I actually picture angels surrounding the audience, floating above them, and I affirm that the God Source is in the room and gives each member of the audience exactly what they need to hear. I envision the audience paying attention and having fun. In my mind I picture the people leaving the presentation with smiles on their faces and their evaluations filled with positive comments about how much they learned and how enjoyable the presentation was for them.

On the days that I begin my presentations this way I can honestly say my affirmative visions seem to come true. On the days I forget to envision these things, the audience seems to be more difficult or restless. They don't seem to warm up to me or bond with me as quickly. I have

15

to work much harder on a physical and emotional level, and my ratings at the end of the sessions are not as high. My sales at the back of the room are not as profitable as they are on the days I affirm and send love in advance to the audience. It's amazing—and true!

The Prayer of Partnership with God

I know that I am one with the Source of my being. I am one with all good things that are coming to me and I am one with the good things I can provide for others. I bless all who come into my life this day, pledging myself to provide the highest service I can to them. My clients, friends, and family respond to me as a beloved partner, giving to me as I give to them. Thank you, my God Source, for the continuing revelation of this perfect law in my life. Amen.

Power Tool Number 3—The Power of Desire and Intention

Everything we know today was a thought before it became a reality. Electricity, flying, computers—all were created in someone's mind before they became manifest in the world. Every great salesperson first made a clear goal to be successful. That is the power of desire and intention. Just think about it. When you intend to do something, you have it fixed in your mind that you are going to do it. Where does intention come from? Intention comes from your desire—to do, to have, to create, or to experience something. One of my purposes in writing this book is to help you see that you co-create your reality with the universe.

Thought is your greatest power to direct and control your life. Thought is real. It is like sunshine, electrical impulses that radiate through your body and out into the world from your mind. Each one of us is a powerful broadcasting station transmitting positive or negative vibrations. And, as we discussed in a previous chapter, your thoughts will attract back to you the same magnetic energy that supports the emotions behind your thoughts. Thus, your thoughts are the most powerful tools you have to direct and control your life. Like an architect's blueprints, your thoughts can help you design and build your future. Buddha said, "All that we are is the result of what we have thought."

You have as many as fifty thousand thoughts a day. That is a tremendous amount of energy. Imagine what kind of energy you could be generating if those were all positive thoughts. Your thoughts could be telling you how courageous you are, or how smart, loving, and creative you are, how you excel at everything you do. You could be telling yourself daily that you can always find solutions to any problems and that life is good. You would be laying the groundwork for a lot of positive actions. There would be no limit to what you could accomplish. When you harness your thought energy and focus it in the direction that you want it to go, you have the power to create your own reality. That is the Power of Desire and Intention.

Control Your Thoughts

As author Napoleon Hill said, "You have absolute control over but one thing—your thoughts . . . This divine prerogative is the sole means by which you may control your destiny. If you fail to control your own mind, you will control nothing else. Your mind is your spiritual estate . . . What you hold in your mind today will shape your experiences of tomorrow."

If you ask truly successful conscious salespeople, they will tell you that having negative opinions about yourself, your product, or service, or even your prospects, will affect your potential to be a really good salesperson. To take charge of your sales success, you must take charge of your thoughts and then the universal law of increase (what you focus on will increase) will work for you.

Begin to take charge of your destiny by thinking of your mind as your personal computer. Here's a very simplistic explanation of how your personal mind-computer works. Think of your brain as having two distinct parts that are under your control. The first, the conscious mind, is the part that is rational, knows right from wrong, directs your thoughts, and makes decisions. This is the part of the mind with which you deliberately create your thoughts. The second part, the subconscious mind, is often called a huge memory bank, for it records everything that you have ever heard, read, seen, or told yourself. Your subconscious mind is said to record every impression that enters your conscious mind through all of your five senses. Your impressions and thoughts are then classified and recorded as references so that they can be recalled through memory.

Your personal sophisticated mind-computer is made of more than just flesh and blood. In fact, you literally have four volts of electricity in your body. Every time you have a thought—good or bad, right or wrong, true or false—those four volts of electricity go from the conscious mind into the subconscious mind. The subconscious mind translates that energy into a reference picture. Our brain thinks in pictures; the objective of the subconscious mind is to match the reference pictures in your mind with the reality that manifests in your daily life. So, all success must be created in the mind before you can create it in reality. Please do note that your subconscious mind doesn't know right from wrong; it simply receives and files the thoughts. It does exactly what your conscious mind tells it to do.

As the most important organ in the body and a highly sophisticated memory bank, the mind works with the data you feed into it every day and with that data it creates the reality of your life. That's why it's so important for you as a salesperson to carefully consider the kind of information you feed your mind. Every thought you think—true or false—travels from the conscious mind and imprints on the subconscious. So, whatever information is programmed into your subconscious about your abilities, your potential, and your self-worth is what you believe to be true. All of this becomes your self-image.

Too often, you don't see your real talents and skills; you simply see the information that has been programmed into your mind-computer from outside sources and your outdated or untrue thoughts. And, because of the universal law of attraction, your self-image—whether real or illusionary—is the foundation upon which your entire future is built. You will simply act out the type of person you conceive yourself to be, based upon your own stored beliefs about yourself.

It's no wonder that some of us fail at sales before we even start. Unless we take charge of the caliber of information that goes into our mind-computer and update our inner pictures, we will be burdened with an outdated self-image and a narrow comfort zone that will not allow us to excel in the sales world. Dr. Maxwell Maltz, in his famous book *Psycho-Cybernetics,* says, "The self-image sets the boundaries of individual accomplishment. It defines what you can and cannot do. Expand the self-image and you expand the areas of the possible."

Research has shown that your nervous system reacts to your mental images in the same way that it reacts to images from the external world. In fact, your nervous system cannot tell the difference between an imagined experience and a real one. In other words, your thoughts actually trigger chemical activity in your brain that your body responds to, whether positive or negative, real or imagined. So, how can you use this knowledge in your daily work to become more successful?

Try this exercise: Close your eyes for a moment and think about the last sales experience you had that was utterly fantastic. Everything went exactly the way you wanted it to go; your client liked you and enjoyed your presentation. They were enthusiastic about your product or service, and they enthusiastically closed the deal right on the spot. Your sales manager made a big deal out of the fact you closed the account. You went home to your loved ones and celebrated what a great day you had and that the commission was going to pay for something you really wanted. As you remember this experience, notice what is happening to your state of mind and to your emotions. You are probably feeling happy, confident, enthusiastic, grateful—and eager to have it happen again! Your body is happily following along behind your thoughts, getting you into the state of feeling good.

Now focus on the last sales call you had that was your worst nightmare. The sales call that was a complete "Murphy's Law" experience. You got caught in traffic and ended up being late. You were in a cell phone dead zone and couldn't call your client. When you arrived, it was clear that the prospect was annoyed at your tardiness. As you made your presentation it was clear that they weren't really interested in anything you had to say. They were continually interrupted and distracted by other things. Finally, ending the meeting, they were rude to you and insulted you and your product. You left the meeting with a bad taste in your mouth about the entire process, and you felt like you had wasted your time. It ruined your whole day.

Again, as you remember the sales call from hell, take note of how you are feeling. What is happening to you right now? What is going on in your body? Maybe you are feeling defeated, angry, and even resentful. Maybe fear enters the picture and your heart starts to pound and your palms begin to sweat. Thoughts of "I'm no good at this" or "who needs this anyway" begin to swirl in your head. Before you know it, you are experiencing all of the feelings that you had at the end of the sales call. You are convinced that selling is too difficult a profession to be in, that the high rate of rejection is too hard to cope with. Just by remembering it, the whole event has become very real again to your body. Your thoughts have taken you there.

Now think about this. If you were going to prepare yourself to meet a brand-new client, which of these two mental exercises would you choose to help you—the positive one or the negative one? You would get better results with the positive one, of course. Know that this is true: Any message you give your subconscious mind on a regular basis will imprint itself and become part of your perception of yourself. Since you are a self-fulfilling prophecy, it behooves you to do as many things as you can to create the image of yourself that you want.

Ralph Waldo Emerson declared, "The ancestor of every action is a thought." If you want to be a conscious and successful salesperson, you have to think of yourself as successful before you actually go on a sales call. Remember the good sales calls as often as possible before you start your day.

Past Programming

As soon as you were born, your mind started taking in information. Your self-image was created very early in your life, somewhere between the age of three and seven. Parents, teachers, peers, society, and the media all helped to program the way your mind views the world and how you see yourself in it. It is important to remember that some of the messages you received may have been negative and self-defeating.

As I described earlier, salespeople are sometimes saddled with some truly awful stereotypes by our culture. In our politically correct world, it is often the businessperson or the salesperson who is chosen as the butt of a joke. All too often it's business people and salespeople who are portrayed as the bad guys. Writers know it's safe to attack us because there is not much we can do. There are no support groups to protest our profession's being abused by the media!

These negative messages, from childhood right up until we embark on our chosen career, can convince us that we are doing something wrong. As I mentioned at the beginning of this book, the world cannot survive without good salespeople to keep the economy strong.

Growing up you probably heard things like "this is a tough world" and "money is the root of all evil." You may have heard "the other guy gets all the breaks," or "I can't win for losing," so often that you have come to believe them on a subconscious level. This kind of thinking sounds the death knell for creativity and prosperity for anyone. It will kill your ability to sell anything if you believe any of these negative messages.

The good news is this: You have the power to override these messages, to program a whole new self-image and a whole new worldview. But in order to do that you have to develop new habits that help limit the amount of negative thinking that goes on in your mind. If you develop a positive, realistic self-image, you discover new capabilities, new talents, and literally turn a life of constant failure into one of consistent success. Decide today to no longer be a victim of the past. Consciously decide to change old negative programs and give yourself a new lease on life. You can do that by maintaining constant awareness about your daily thoughts.

Taking Charge of Your Mind

One basic technique that will enable you to create more positive thoughts and actions in your selling career is simple, but it will have a tremendous impact on your career—not only on how you do your job but on the results you get, as well.

What's the first thing you do when you get up in the morning? Most of us pour a cup of coffee, and read, watch, or listen to the news. Right off the bat you load up your mind-computer with murder, terrorism, and financial doom and gloom. The news reliably bombards you with hundreds of reasons to be afraid of the world and to discourage yourself from believing that you can succeed. It is important not to allow this type of negative information into your mind first thing in the morning. Nothing can squelch creativity faster or darken a positive attitude more effectively than negative news.

Life in a sales career is ever-changing, so a *conscious* salesperson's means of moving through it must also be dynamic. A conscious salesperson knows that it is important to constantly scan the landscape of life, looking for opportunities and new ways to serve people. Further, you have to be ready and willing to take action on those opportunities. When we buy into the hype of sensational and negative sound bytes peddled by the media, we unknowingly limit our opportunities for creative thinking. We actually block our ability to think positively about ourselves, the coming day, our products or services; to discover new territories; or to forge new business relationships.

Think about it: More millionaires were created during the Great Depression than at any other time in history. Do you know why? The people who became successful did not spend their time listening to all the reports about the infamous "poor economy." They did not let negative news control their future. They acted like entrepreneurs. These true entrepreneurs believed in themselves and were willing to take calculated risks. They looked for opportunities and found low prices, low-cost labor, and government funding. They made tremendous amounts of money because they took charge of their own destiny through their thoughts and their actions!

A few years ago I started a coaching program called The Millionaire Mindset Program. I studied how people became rich. I knew that the more I focused on the secrets of becoming wealthy and acted on those principles, the more likely that I would be able to make my own dreams come true. And the more I studied successful people, the wealthier I became because I learned from their positive mindsets and imitated their actions. Becoming independently wealthy was my clear desire and intention. Today, as I present my coaching program to entrepreneurs and business owners, I can speak with authority that the strategies actually work every time.

In order to effectively use the Power of Desire and Intention in your life you have to clear away your negative mental debris and stop allowing others' fear-based thoughts to affect you. To do this, exercise number one is: Stop reading the newspaper or listening to the news first thing in the morning unless it is directly related to your own business success. Simply modifying unnecessary negative news intake will clear the way for you to begin each day with enthusiasm for your work and will allow you to reap huge rewards.

In order to become more successful in sales, you have to be productive and creative. You can't do that if you reinforce your fears and doubts before you even begin your day. Now, I am not saying stick your head in the sand and don't find out what is going on in the world each day, but you do not have to let the news determine your attitude and frame of mind. You must take charge of the caliber of information that you allow into your mind if you want to control the caliber of your daily thoughts. You must focus only on information that assists you, not on that which puts you in an unresourceful frame of mind.

Of course, you will still want to enjoy your morning rituals but your assignment is to read something inspirational or motivational—something that lifts up your spirit and encourages you to believe in yourself. Read or listen to something that will help you think creatively about the sales calls you have to make during the coming day. One of the fastest tracks to success is to control the quality of what goes on in your brain. Face it, if you don't take it upon yourself to limit negative information, who will?

Negative Mind Talk

After your morning ritual, what is the next thing you usually do? The shower. You go into the bathroom, stop and take a peak in the mirror, and it starts. Your brain starts a conversation with you. If you are lucky it will start on a high note. With thoughts like, "Those clients at the Johnson account are going to be thrilled with my proposal." You pat yourself on the back; tell yourself how hard you have worked and what a great job you have done. If this is your scenario, you are on your way to a great day.

If, on the other hand, your mind is not in such a good mood, the conversation might go something like this: "Man, you look tired." You respond with, "Well, I wouldn't look so tired if I didn't have to work so hard and my sales manager would give me some good leads." Your mind says, "My account list is not big enough and the competition is killing me." And so it goes; before you know it you don't even want to go to work. You're dreading the entire day ahead of you. It's time to hit the Cancel Button on your negative thoughts.

The Cancel Button is a technique you can use to reprogram all of your negative thoughts. Every time a negative thought comes into your mind, stop and say, "Wait, I know what to do about this." Then, mentally press the Cancel Button to delete the thought. Of course, as soon as you do that another negative thought will pop into your mind— unless you replace it first with something positive. For example, if your mind says to you, "I wish I didn't have to call on Thomas Electronics today." You can say, "Oops, time for the Cancel Button," and in your mind you deliberately punch the button. While you are doing that, though, you must create a new positive thought in your head. So, you say to yourself, "I am going to be at the top of my game when I call on the Thomas people today."

Don't be afraid to use your Cancel Button wherever you go, especially in the beginning. When you first start using it you will find yourself hitting it all day long. That's okay. Negative thoughts are tenacious and you have to work at getting rid of them. Let it be a game you play with yourself. In a very short time you will see that positive thinking is becoming easier and soon it will even become a habit. This might feel like a silly little exercise at first, but it works very well. Try it; your success depends on the caliber of thinking that goes on in your mind. A Cancel Button can help you get on the road to successful thinking.

What you are really doing by using this simple tool called Cancel Button is a "pattern interrupt" to change the focus of your thoughts. Remember, what you focus on continues, so if you are smart, you will want to stop the destructive cycle of negative programming as soon as possible. When your actions or performance does not meet your expectations, don't belittle yourself with negative self-talk. This type of response will only perpetuate the poor performance you did not want, and add to the negative programming. You must replace those images of yourself that do not create value in your life and which you certainly do not want to continue. You will find that using this new tool will empower you to focus your subconscious mind on new and positive messages or programs.

Many salespeople invest in their own failure by browbeating themselves when they get a "no" in the sales process, further destroying their self-esteem. You don't allow others to talk to you with such poison, so why are you doing it to yourself?

As a salesperson, you judge yourself more than anyone else. For example, how many times have you caught yourself saying, "I never have enough time in the day to get everything done?" Now think about what you are programming yourself to be—always behind! In the future, instead of reinforcing the negative habit, say to yourself, "Cancel. That's not like me to worry. I have all the time I need each day to be effective."

Using this technique only once obviously won't keep you from worrying or help you instantly reprogram yourself for total success in the future. The statements of success must be consciously and repeatedly programmed into your life over a period of time for the information to be assimilated. Your brain's computer must digest and absorb the new program. When you use this technique, you are literally using the four volts of electrical energy in your brain to create a new program.

Everyone knows you can't harvest apples from a pear tree; similarly, you can't think thoughts of lack and reap success and prosperity in the sales world. Remember, we can only act in a manner that matches our mind-computer's pictures of who we think we are and what we think we can do. You have the power to reprogram yourself with new information that will assist you in achieving your goals. You're not stuck with old mindsets. If you've told yourself negative things about yourself, or other people have told you negative things, then start today to reprogram your thoughts with positive messages and self-talk.

Shakespeare's Hamlet observed, "There is nothing either good or bad, but thinking makes it so." Let's review what we know about your mind and its thought programming:

- Your subconscious mind acts like a computer.
- All thoughts, fears, and emotions send mental pictures from the conscious mind through the nervous system to the subconscious, and the body prepares to act on the request. (Remember the four volts of electricity?)
- The subconscious part of the mind, like the earth, simply reproduces what is planted in it. If you have unhealthy thoughts and emotions about imagined fears, worry, resentment, or guilt, the mind–body responds with a tense feeling of nervousness, stress-related illness, tiredness, and lack of energy and creativity.
- Your subconscious mind produces whatever you focus on. This powerful mind-computer doesn't care what information you put in; it simply acts on all information as if it were true.

I am going to suggest several daily morning exercises that you can use to develop an open frame of mind and positively focus your thinking. I promise you, as a salesperson you will see miracles happen in your life if you try these simple exercises. Feel free to expand, change, and improve the way you ask for help daily from your Source.

Spiritual Morning Exercises

As I already discussed, you can fully utilize your success potential when you decide to take responsibility for the caliber of information you put into your mind and to get clear about what intentions and goals you want to set for yourself. As a salesperson, I have tried different techniques over the years to put myself in the best state of mind to be successful, but these seem to work best for me. Notice, too, that I also ask for God's assistance. As the Christian Bible promises, "Ask and it shall be given you, seek and ye shall find, knock and the door shall be opened." If your desires are not definitive, it's very hard for your God Source to give you the innovative ideas, directions, or answers to create the lifestyle you want for yourself.

Prosperity is the result of deliberate thought and action. When you read about historically prominent and successful people, you will find that most of them use a technique for creating their desires—they write down what they want. I believe there is magic in putting ideas on paper. We have to acknowledge the fact that we are deliberate creators: our thoughts and actions create our life.

Your To-Do List

Start a new daily ritual by sitting down, first thing in the morning, and listing your goals for that day. Write down only the things that you are planning to act on today, or this week. The purpose of this exercise is to focus clearly. It is a very effective way of invoking the creative Power of Desire and Intention. By focusing your attention at the beginning of every day on what you want to do with your life energy, you give your computer (your brain) direction, and it always follows the most powerful and emotion-driven directions given to it. By simply taking a couple of minutes first thing in the morning to make a list of your desired accomplishments, you'll be in control of your day. By spending your life energy wisely you are giving yourself a wonderful gift—a new lease on life. Before you know it, this new strategy will put you in control of your life. After you have written your personal to-do list, it's time to go for big assistance by asking God to help you.

God's To-Do List

Make a list that you would like the universe to act upon. This is important to do so you can clearly identify your desires. This exercise allows you to define an intention and then let God handle the details of bringing it to you. The universe has the ability to arrange details and circumstances much better than you. Your job is to clearly define what it is you want, to envision it clearly, and then be alert enough to see it when it presents itself to you! God will handle bringing you the knowledge, people, and opportunities necessary to accomplish your goals. Include on this list anything you are unable to act on immediately, either because you don't know how to get started, or because you don't have the time and resources to support it.

In case you have never created a God's To-Do List, I'll share one of mine so you can see how easy it is. By simply getting clear about what you want to happen during your day, you will be ready to see the opportunities when they are presented to you. Let me give you an example of my God's To-Do List:

- Attract the perfect staff to my office. People who are honest, hard-working, creative, have initiative, and are motivated. Attract people for my team that I am thrilled to have working with me.
- Handle all the details to bring harmony and peace to my neighborhood.
- Lead me to the perfect vendors whom I will love and who can handle all the big projects my office has planned this year.
- Attract to me the information, skills, and knowledge to assist my clients.
- Attract to me only the clients and customers whom I am best suited to serve and to whom I can give the highest and best value.
- Attract to me only honest and easy-to-get-along-with clients and customers, who value me and who are appreciative of my services.

Trust that God will hear you loud and clear. Your God Source will start to deliver your desires to you in ways you could never have dreamed. And, since you took the time to be clear about what you wanted, you'll recognize the opportunities as they come to you.

Prayer for Clear Desire and Intentions

In this moment I know that I am a positive, powerful being, clear on my desires and purposeful in my intentions. The universe and my mind-body arrange for me to receive my every need and desire, and they come to me in wonderful ways.
And so it is.

Power Tool Number 4—
The Power of Detachment

Closing a sale can feel like the fourth of July, Christmas, and your birthday all rolled into one. That's why salespeople are so eager to make it happen. Over the years hundreds of "closing" techniques have been developed to help you close a sale.

But what happens when you have done the best you can, when you have been as helpful as you can be, and you still can't close the deal? Then what? Detach? Let go? No way! Most salespeople are convinced they have to hang on till the bitter end, that the only way they can succeed at closing a sale is by enforcing their will. At that point, making the sale has become a personal thing, as though the transaction is about the salesperson in a personal way. And the typical salesperson is very attached to the outcome of a sales event, wouldn't you say?

In sales, one of the most underused spiritual principles is to be detached from the outcome of your efforts. One of the greatest causes of suffering is attachment. The more easily you can let go of the old and embrace the new, the more quickly you can prosper rather than struggle in life.

When you make a sales presentation, you know you must do your best, be professional, timely, and attentive to the customer's needs, wants, and desires. After you have done the very best presentation possible, you have to let it go. Do not be mentally and emotionally attached to the outcome of the sales event. Release thoughts and feelings about whether the client will complete the sale. Move the energy of your thoughts and feelings toward preparing your mental picture of a successful sales event with your next client.

The truth is that if you are attached to the outcome of a sales event, the heightened emotion of fearing the loss of the sale can repel the very thing you want the most. Being attached to the outcome will actually foster fear, frustration, self-pity, self-recrimination, and even anger. Hanging on to a sale repels it; once you release it, you must truly trust that either it will come back to you or something better will take its place. As you learn to work with these spiritual power tools, you will learn to trust that nothing ever leaves your life unless something better is coming, so there's no need to feel attached to the outcome of any one sales event!

Having attachments takes a great deal of life energy and drains you of creative proactive energy. Once you become anxious that you need to make a sale you can sabotage it by pushing too hard or acting a little needy. On a subconscious level, that needy feeling will affect the sale. Physically, you may not recognize that you are acting needy, but the emotional "charge" of even subconscious needy feelings will repel the very thing you are after.

Buyers are attracted to confidence. They want to "go with winners" because they like to see the winner in themselves. Needy, greedy, and grasping people are not winners. Trust me, your buyer's emotional radar detector can sense if you are attached to making a sale. If your buyer feels your need for the sale, the product or service feels less attractive.

Detachment is not disinterest. You must remain attached to the customer's needs without being attached to the outcome of the sales event. Detachment creates an atmosphere of freedom in a sales call—the freedom for right action to occur. What's right for the salesperson is not always right for the customer. First and foremost, conscious salespeople want outcomes that are in the highest and best interest of their customers, because, in the long run, that is the focus that achieves the salesperson's goals, too.

One of the greatest challenges of spiritual growth is learning to release old ways of doing things. Release beliefs, people, and things that no longer serve you. Bless them as they leave, and embrace the new as it comes. Letting go is an important aspect of growing spiritually. As a conscious salesperson, accept that new growth involves learning new skills, making changes, and creating new attitudes.

Just before I went into the public speaking business, I was in commercial real estate. Interest rates were sky-high for commercial loans at that time and I was not selling anything. I was forced to face myself and admit that I really did not like selling commercial real estate. It was a great job for the folks in my office who loved it, but I did not. By not being successful I was forced to ask myself what I really wanted to do with my life. I talk about this time in my life in great detail in my *Success Is an Inside Job.*

The bottom line is, I gave up my ego and my attachment to becoming successful in commercial real estate. I let that career go and jumped into the speaking business and now all I can say is "thank you, God." I found my real calling in life. If I had not let go of my attachment to my old career I might never have found my true passion and life's work.

Start practicing nonattachment by observing your own thoughts and actions. In what situations do you feel an attachment to the outcome? Who and what are you attached to? Practice giving up your attachment one situation at a time.

As you grow spiritually, you must give up your dependence on your attachments. You will notice one day that you are happy without them, and then you are free. Then the objects of your attachments (such as a certain dollar value of commissions) can be in your life without your being controlled by them.

To be a conscious salesperson you must realize that your well-being is never really contingent on what someone else does or does not do. Your well-being is always your conscious choice. When trying to be of service and make a sale, you must trust the process and release any desperate feelings. The old saying that the universe is perfect and there are no failures is true. Give yourself the gift of detaching from your worries and fears about making a sale and trust that everything is in divine order.

My first real sales job was in broadcast radio and I was so excited about it that the sales seemed to happen like magic. With no experience and no expectations, I was so enthusiastic that I sold almost everyone I called on in the beginning. I was really doing well.

My sales manager at the time believed the theory that the more salespeople were in debt, the more motivated they would be to make sales. At my sales manger's urging I got an expensive new car, lots of new business suits, and a much bigger apartment. Suddenly I was deeply in debt and the pressure was intense to make more money. I did not realize it at the time, but his mindset of motivation-by-debt backfired on me!

With every call, I now felt pressure to make the sale. Before getting in debt, when I made sales calls I had been having fun, talking to people and sharing success stories about how my product would benefit them. I was not overly concerned about whether this prospect would buy because I knew that I had a good product and that I would always have interested customers. Suddenly all these big bills were coming in each month and my only focus was my desperate need to make more sales to cover my bills.

The more I needed to make a sale because the rent was due, the less interested people seemed to be in my product, and I was confused. I was selling the same product, working harder and longer, and yet making fewer sales. What had happened?

I was lucky enough to have a spiritual advisor. In desperation I went to her and told her my story. She explained to me the law of detachment. She said I had a few options to change my luck but the best one was to become partners with God in my business. She shared with me the exercise of praying for my clients and putting their well-being over mine. She also explained to me how important it was that I not be held hostage by material things. I was not happy at the time about downsizing my life to get it under control, but that gave me the freedom of not having to make a specific dollar level of sales.

Even today, after all these years, I still live beneath my means and that has always given me a sense of freedom. I will never have to do anything I don't want to do just because of money. By detaching from a requirement to have certain material goods, I can choose to keep my business affairs in integrity with myself and others. Please don't get me wrong, I still live very well. I am wealthy because I have put the interests of my clients above my own needs and, in turn, that continuous thought pattern has attracted more clients to me than I can work with.

God's Got It in Escrow

Here's an exercise to help you get out of your own way and allow for results that are right for everyone. This exercise will assist you in trusting that the universe will bring about the right and perfect actions. You can give up feeling out of control and desperate for sales.

As you start your day or workweek, make your list of prospects whom you will be talking to or calling on. Before you contact your prospects, take the time to envision God going forward to assist you with your clients' needs. Send your prospects love and light. Ask for only the highest and best good for each prospect or client. Affirm that you will receive the God Source's help during this day to be resourceful, knowledgeable of your subject, curious, open-minded, and of highest integrity, and that you will attract the people who are the perfect fit for your product or service. Use your imagination to see that you will easily supply them with whatever satisfies their needs, wants, and desires.

Next, release your work to the God Source and go about your business feeling relaxed, knowing that all is in divine order. The perfect appointments at the perfect time are being made for you. You are inspired to call on the right people to satisfy their needs at perfect times when they need your products or services. Send love, light, and appreciation to all the people that you meet and serve. Ask your God Source to now handle all objections, fears, doubts, and negative influences. Affirm that the perfect sales are made and that you are relaxed in the knowledge that a greater power is working on your behalf and on behalf of your customers.

But remember, you must *ask for help* before help is delivered. This exercise will assist you in detaching from the outcomes of your earnest endeavors. You will come to know that the Universe arranges details and circumstances much better than you ever could. Your job is to clearly define what you want and thank your God Source for bringing it to you. Your God Source will bring you the knowledge, people, and opportunities necessary to accomplish your goals.

Let me give you an example of my God's Got It in Escrow list.

Dear God,

Thank you for sending your light into all my sales appointments. Thank you for attracting to me only the clients and customers to whom I can give the highest and best value. Thank you for attracting to me easy-to-get-along-with clients and customers who value me and who are appreciative of my services. Thank you for handling all the details of being able to serve my clients with the best service possible and for bringing to me all the help, resources, and support I need to be of service to them. Thank you for always creating a win-win situation for all concerned. Thank you for inspiring me to call on only these people to whom I can be of service. Inspire me to listen to my intuition on the correct timing of calling on clients.

Know that by thanking your God Source before you actually receive the blessings you are accepting your good in the present moment. This works because, energetically speaking, there is no future, there is only now. You are a co-creator with your God Source. Trust that It hears you loud and clear and will start to deliver your desires to you in ways you could never have dreamed.

Energetically speaking, the past is a locked door and cannot be changed, and the future is made up of the emotional thought energy you utilize in this moment. When you declare your intentions to the God Source and impress your subconscious with heightened expectancy of the good you desire, you open the way for the manifestation of it to appear in your life.

If you will try this exercise for just 30 days, you will find that it will be easier to get appointments and your time will be better utilized. Your prospects will bond with you faster and trust you more. You will experience more sales and more joy while selling. Your prospects will respect you more and give you more referrals. All of these blessings will happen when you take the time to join forces with your God Source to pave the way before you.

Don't take Lee Milteer's word for anything. Experiment with this exercise yourself and analyze your own results. You can do this!

Don't Take Anything Personally

As the old saying goes, "Sticks and stones may break your bones but words can never hurt you." When you are in sales, rejection is a part of your daily life. As a conscious salesperson, the best tool you could ever possess is how to detach from a prospect's rejection—to not take it personally. You see, the very personal fear of being rejected is actually the fear of not being good enough. You must detach your self-concept from others' opinions about you, your product, or your company.

If you take other people's words and actions personally, you are doomed before you start a sales call because internally you feel like a victim. If you get rejected, a part of you is saying, "Poor me, I am not good enough; I am not intelligent enough; I am not attractive enough; I am not worthy." These are damaging and false beliefs. What do they do to your creative energy? They squash it!

We judge and punish ourselves for not living up to our own arbitrary image of perfection. No one is ever going to be perfect. By not being perfect we often reject ourselves. We wear social masks to keep others from seeing the real us. Deep down we feel inauthentic and don't accept ourselves. We are our own worst judges. Trying to be perfect is unnatural and destructive to our souls, going against the spiritual concept that you are a perfect child of God.

It takes a great deal of courage to challenge your own beliefs about rejection and perfection. Accept that thoughts of insufficiency are fear-based and that they waste your personal creative energy and power. Use your energy to change those thoughts and you'll change the feelings behind them, reclaiming your personal power.

A massive amount of freedom and energy comes to you when you take nothing personally. You become immune to negative people and negative situations and to rejection of any kind. Understanding the game of life, you simply go forth and do not let anything bother you.

You know that your connection to the God Source is never broken and no one has the power to hurt you unless you let them. Do not give your power away to others—*ever!* Detach from other people's world. You live in your own world.

Let's play with this concept. Let's pretend you are in the middle of a sales call, making your presentation, and the prospect says something insulting or demeaning, or simply rejects your offer. To keep your creative energy flowing, your thoughts should be something like this:

It has nothing to do with me personally. Maybe it's spillover from something else I don't know about. Maybe she just had an argument and is still angry. Or maybe she's in physical pain and feeling too overwhelmed to make a new decision. Maybe my product is not right for her budget or she was not really interested to begin with.

Who knows? It's not your job to explain a personal rejection. It's your job to find out if your product or service is really a good match to your client at this time. It's your job to review your presentation to discover whether your product or service really fits her needs. It's your job to leave the client with the feeling that she would purchase from you at some time in the future if she had the need to do so.

When I was a sales representative for a radio station in Norfolk, Virginia, I was assigned a new client who was the owner of a statewide chain of retail stores. I had talked to the owner several times on the phone before I met with him in person. We had gotten along really well and seemed to be on track to do a lot of business together. I walked into his office and just about three minutes into my presentation he cut me off and told me he had changed his mind and did not want to advertise with my radio station. Then he told me not to call on him ever again. He couldn't get rid of me fast enough. I was stunned! Not only could I not figure out what I had done wrong, I was very disappointed not to make the sale that I had worked on for months. I replayed every word that had been said over and over in my mind. I tried hard to figure out what on earth went wrong.

Nothing like that had ever happened to me before and I was in shock from his in-person rejection of me. I was very upset and allowed the encounter to damage my confidence and self-esteem. It took me several weeks to get over the feeling of unworthiness and rejection. My sales declined and I lost my enthusiasm about my ability to sell radio advertising. I finally went to my sales manager, a very wise man, who said to me, "So what! You cannot win them all and who knows what his problem is. We know you, Lee, and you are a good salesperson. Don't let this one rejection upset you. Just say to yourself, 'Next client!' and move on to the next prospect that you can assist with their advertising needs. Hey, the truth is he needs us more than we need him."

Turns out, I ran into this man a few months later at a chamber of commerce meeting in my hometown. We ended up sitting in the same row in the audience and he had to walk past me to get to his seat. When I saw him I recalled all the pain I had suffered over his rejection. After the presentation, as I was leaving for the day, he came over to me and offered an apology to me. He said, "Lee, I have to tell you that you did nothing wrong in my office the day you visited me. You were quite professional, in fact. The problem was that, when I was looking at you, I could not stop thinking about my soon-to-be ex-wife. The truth was, I couldn't look at you without thinking of how angry I was with her. I guess I took out my anger on you." He continued, "You even had the exact same type of eyeglasses and I couldn't bear to be in the room with you. I'm sorry I mistreated you due to my emotional pain."

I could never have guessed that this was the problem that lost me the sale. I had long since let it go and stopped taking it personally because I knew in my heart I had been completely professional. So, it just goes to show, you can never know what is going on in someone else's head and heart.

I have a number of resource books that I use on a regular basis to keep me conscious, and one of my favorites is *The Four Agreements: A Practical Guide to Personal Freedom.* The author, Don Miguel Ruiz, says, "Personal importance, or taking things personally, is the maximum expression of selfishness because we make the assumption that everything is about 'me.'" Ruiz continues, "Nothing other people do is because of you. It is because of themselves. All people live in their own dream, in their own mind; they are in a completely different world from the one we live in. When we take something personally, we make the assumption that they know what is in our world, and we try to impose our world on their world."

In the sales world, even though a situation may seem very personal to you, it may really have nothing to do with you at all. When others offer their opinions, the truth is they are coming from their own programming and feelings, beliefs, and view of life.

As salespeople, we do not have to let others' opinions be part of our inner world. People's opinions are simply the way they see the world. Nothing they think about you has anything to do with you, really. They see you from their own beliefs using their own lens. If someone is upset with you, the truth is they are really upset with themselves—you just provide a point of focus for them to let it go.

For example, I recently found myself annoyed with my mate because his home office was an out-of-control mess. Later, I admitted to myself that by being annoyed with him I took the focus off the very annoying fact that *my* office was a mess. I had to admit that I was really angry with myself for not being more organized in my own life. It was easier to lash out at him than to face my own disorganization. I had moved the focus off myself and projected my anger at him. It was my office mess that I was truly mad at, not his!

As a conscious salesperson, understand that you have to trust yourself and choose to believe or not to believe what someone says to you. You must trust yourself to make the right choices of what to believe in. If you feel rejected, ask yourself, "Am I taking this personally? Why? This situation has nothing to do with me at all." Give up guilt or self-judgment and follow your heart.

You can lose the fear of being ridiculed or rejected by others and stay in a state of joy and happiness by simply understanding that you are never responsible for the actions of others. You are only responsible for yourself. When you refuse to take anything personally, you cannot be hurt by the comments or actions of other people. No matter what some-one says or does, you can still follow your heart and soul and recognize that you are the divine child of God.

Prayer of Detachment

I AM AT PEACE.

I am God's perfect Child. I don't take anything personally. I am at peace. I am undisturbed. I believe in the power of God in my life and there is no power in conditions or personalities unless I give them power. Nothing can upset or disturb me. I feel nothing done against me. I allow all souls to be on their own path and learn their own lessons. I give them permission to have their own opinions. Nothing in my past or future can hurt me. I trust the Divine Law of Life to take care of all my needs. I now trust the Infinite Wisdom of God working in and through me to bring me my good. I am undisturbed and always at peace.

So be it.

Power Tool Number 5—The Power of Truth, Integrity, and High Ethics

How important is truth in today's world? One of the biggest misconceptions about salespeople is that we will say anything to make a sale. To the public, and sometimes to ourselves, it appears that the end objective is more important than telling the truth. That is just not true for the conscious salesperson. Our job is to find the benefits and value of our product or service for our prospects and tell them the truth.

When it comes to making a sale, what are your ethics? You can have average ethics and give the customer fair exchange for their money, no less, no more, which is how the average salesperson operates. A conscious salesperson wants to operate from maximum ethics, where you don't just ask how to get more sales but how to give more and better service to your clients. When you offer exceptional service, you impress your clients with more than they expected. One of the best reasons to employ maximum ethical standards and behavior in sales is simply peace of mind.

Dan Kennedy, a mentor and friend of mine for many years, has written many business and sales books. I recommend all of his materials. In his *NO B.S. Business Success* book, Dan suggests that maintaining integrity and high ethics is one of the most important aspects of long-term success.

He says, "Personal faith is not usually a topic entrepreneurs discuss openly, but just about every highly successful person I've ever known has a very definite set of spiritual beliefs and, as a result, acts with faith. For me, faith is based on four simple ideas:

1. There is a plan and purpose behind our lives.
2. We're here to learn some things and to accomplish some things.
3. We were intended and are invited to live prosperously.
4. When operating within certain parameters, we have every reason to expect positive results."

He goes on to say, "This solid expectation of positive results empowers you to cut through the clutter and confusion of self-doubt, fear, criticism, cynicism, negativism, and other obstacles." The point here is that when you pursue your goals as a salesperson, they must be achieved by enriching others, not at the expense of others. You must accept responsibility for your own actions.

William F. James, founder of Boys Town, Missouri, said that there are only three things necessary to success: first, normal intelligence; second, determination; and third, absolute honesty. One cannot be a little honest; it's all the way or nothing.

Know Your Personal Truth

The problem is that most people really don't know their own personal truth. As kids we were taught always to tell the truth and that honesty was the best policy. The bad news is that kids watch adults lie and get away with it all the time on television, in the movies, and in real life. Kids notice that often, when you tell the truth, it can upset people and you might even get punished.

Since most people want to avoid conflict and confrontation, we get in the habit of not telling the truth to avoid any upset it may cause. The truth gets told only when it is to our advantage to share it. Without realizing it, we sometimes don't tell the truth just so we can fit in with society's expectations. As salespeople, we have sometimes stretched the truth to make the sale.

The serious consequence of inconsistent truth telling is the resulting blurring of moral and ethical lines. When we lose our morals and ethics, which are our own personal truth, we actually lose the essence of ourselves. As spiritual beings, when we stop telling the truth, we lose integrity with ourselves. If you cannot trust yourself you cannot trust anyone. This sad state of affairs will never bring you peace of mind or happiness, much less success!

To truly become a conscious salesperson you have to stop worrying about what others will think of you if you speak your truth in an appropriate manner. If you really want to live an authentic life and be proud of yourself and your sales profession, you must not let anyone tell you who you are or what your truth should be. It's important for you to know your own truth and to speak your own truth. Become truly who you are and act only from what you truly believe. If you don't believe in what you are selling, you will never be truly successful at selling it.

Yes, I know it's easier to go with the flow than to stand your ground when problems occur. But after a while, if you don't stand your ground, you won't even know what you believe or think.

Our society and the media feed us an enormous amount of "shoulds" every day. We are told what we should like and should not like, how to think and how to fit in so that the "majority" accepts us. As of today, wake up and realize that, though it might be difficult to speak your truth at first, you will have more respect for yourself if you do. And once you get in touch with your own personal truth, you will not allow others to walk on it.

It's important to take back your power in life and understand that you do not have to conform to what everyone else is thinking or doing. You have the power and responsibility to decide what you believe, what your personal truth is, and how to stand within that truth. Be proud to be an individual.

When I urge you to speak your truth please do not let that be an invitation to be offensive or difficult or even to feel that you have to defend your own truth. As a conscious salesperson, always speak your truth with kindness and love. Who you are speaks loudly without words.

Understand that you may not always agree with others and that each individual has his own personal truth. No one has to agree with yours or join you in that truth. Realize that, once you let your own real truth come out, people around you might be upset that you are no longer "playing the game." You cannot control others and the good news is that they no longer can control you.

Do you know your own personal truth? Often in social situations I hear people give their opinion about certain subjects, yet I know it's really not their opinion. I know they are repeating what they have heard from others and have not taken the time to know what they really think or feel about a subject. People tend to look at just one side of a subject and then parrot back in a conversation what they think other people want to hear and will find acceptable.

When I was very young and unconscious about who I really was, I found myself trying to be all things to all people. If I was around a set of people who thought one way, I found myself agreeing with them. Yet in the same day I could be around another set of opinions and agree with them, too, just to be part of the group. I had no clue as to who I was or what I believed. It was easier for me just to go along with the crowd of the moment. Thankfully, I moved toward a quest for truly knowing who I am and what I personally stand for and believe.

Do some soul searching and ask yourself some life-defining questions. It takes a great deal of courage to examine your own beliefs. Do you really just want to follow the masses and believe what the media spoon-feeds you? Question your own beliefs about what feels right to you and how you want to live your life. I recommend *The Hard Questions for an Authentic Life*, by Susan Piver, as resource book for your personal investigation. Piver's *Questions* can help you sift through your beliefs so you know what you want to keep and what you want to discard.

To begin to define your own truth, you might go into a quiet place, maybe out in nature. Get centered (quiet your mind) and ask yourself some soul-searching questions to help define what your truth is for you as an individual. This won't keep you from being open-minded to new views on life, but it will help you to know your personal truth, how to operate in the world in the way that is authentic for you.

Are you aware of it when you are not operating from your own personal truth or ethic? Keep in mind that living from your personal truth involves not only how you feel you ought to be treated, but also how you treat or protect others. For example, a family member says something untrue or negative about another family member. You keep quiet and don't correct the error—a breach of personal ethics. Or another salesperson takes over one of your accounts and you don't speak up about it—a breach of business ethics. Say you are in a social setting and someone keeps making sexist jokes or racist comments and you think, "That doesn't have anything to do with me and they're not talking about me so I'll keep quiet"—a breach of personal ethics.

I suggest that you write your observations about your personal truth investigation in a notebook or journal. Write about the topics in your life that you talk about but haven't really clearly defined for yourself. Write about topics such as sales, work, money, success, love, spirituality, nature, politics, war, poverty, marriage, children, homelessness. Add subjects as they come along in your daily life.

When someone asks you how you feel on a subject, really think about it before you speak. Don't just repeat what you have heard others say about the subject. If you don't know how you feel about something, simply state, "I don't know. I'll have to think about that." Then do take the time to think about it and discover your truth about it. Remember that in business it's more important to be respected than liked. Needless to say, when you are in sales, it is smart not to discuss subjects that are truly hot topics, those that hardly anyone agrees on, such as politics, sex, and religion.

As a conscious salesperson, do your best to speak your truth with kindness and avoid defensiveness. You don't have to defend yourself when you live from your authentic truth. Everyone has their own personal truth and no one has to agree with yours. You cannot control others and you don't want them controlling you.

Be Impeccable with Your Word

A book that has made a huge impact on me and that I recommend to everyone is *The Four Agreements*, by Don Miguel Ruiz. In the chapter called "Be Impeccable with Your Word" he says, "Your word is the power that you have to create. Your word is the gift that comes directly from God. The Gospel of John in the Bible, speaking of the creation of the universe, says, 'In the beginning was the Word, and the Word was with God, and the Word was God.'"

Your word is the most powerful tool you have as a human being and as a conscious salesperson. Like a sword with two edges, your word can create positive experiences or destroy your peace of mind. This concept of being impeccable is very important for us as conscious salespeople because we live by our honor. We honor ourselves by living true to our word, so our word needs to be reliable.

Unwittingly, our culture has allowed the negative habit of lying to persist in much of our interpersonal and public communication. The word "impeccability" means "without sin." It is said that a sin is anything that you do which goes against your true self. Any type of lying is certainly going against your true self.

Ruiz says in his book that when you are impeccable, you take responsibility for your actions, but you do not judge or blame yourself. He also says that sin begins with rejection of yourself and that self-rejection is the greatest sin (error) we can commit.

When I read that last statement—that self-rejection is the biggest sin you can commit—I had to sit with it for a while. I finally came to understand that lying is self-rejection. As Ruiz says, speaking the truth is the most important part of being impeccable with your word. Only the truth sets you free.

Stop Gossiping

If you want to be conscious about your actions and impeccable with your words, you must delete gossiping from your personal habits. It's true that misery loves company and perhaps that's what has made gossiping a major social problem in our society today. Since our word is power, every time we spread negative information we are contributing to the pain and suffering of others. Go on a gossip-free diet for 30 days and notice the difference in your relationships with other people.

Again, focus on what is good in life instead of what is not working, for yourself and for others in your life. Your attitude and productivity will improve and, since all energy gets results, you will change your life's results because you are focusing on others' good. Use your time to write out your goals and think about them, rather than to entertain yourself and others with gossip.

Have Integrity with Yourself

I work as a speaker, coach, and consultant for organizations of all sizes, from small to huge. I am proud to say that once I am hired I am often asked to come back to work with the groups over and over again. One of the signs of success is when people want more of you.

I started getting feedback from my clients who said that after my presentation, the number of people quitting their jobs went up. Since I have long-term repeat contracts with many of these organizations, they obviously love my work but understandably do not want their employees leaving! They asked me to leave out of my presentation the part about "if you are not happy here, if you do not love this job, you should leave after giving reasonable notice." I was torn about what to do in this situation. I work for and get paid by the clients who employ these people, and I have a moral obligation to supply them with the teaching materials we have agreed upon. On the other hand, if I don't offer the "love it or leave it" information to their employees, whom I have been asked to teach to think at a higher level and to be aware of their options, I would lack integrity.

I explained to my clients the real truth: that employers are much better off without employees who are unhappy and don't want to be there. There it is, *truth*, simple and to the point. It is best for a company's long-term health to weed out the weakest links in the chain. In this instance, I stayed true to my highest integrity and was rewarded with the creative energy to find a win-win situation for all concerned.

Fire Clients Who Do Not Honor You

Another area where the truth can set you free is to "fire" outrageous, difficult, or dishonest clients, those who will never be happy with you no matter what you do. You may be thinking, "Fire clients, what is spiritual or successful about that? Aren't I supposed to turn the other cheek?" The answer is: When you have done your best, when nothing is working and they are still unhappy, it's time to let them go.

When you stay in a false stage of hope that the difficult prospect will change, you are giving away time and energy that you could be using to work with people who want to do business with you. These people are doing much damage to your self-esteem and well-being. The definition of insanity is doing the same thing over and over again and hoping for a new result. When you work with a client who disrespects you, is impossible to please, and who gives you emotional distress, it's time to FIRE the client.

You don't hear many salespeople talk about this subject of firing clients but, as a conscious salesperson, you must honor yourself, your time, and your peace of mind if you want to offer the best service possible. Develop your sense of observation so that you can identify early on when you are in a no-win situation. There are always red flags if you are conscious enough to look for them and acknowledge them when you see them.

When I fire a customer, what I am really doing is calling a "creative halt" on that account. I am no longer going to squander my creative energies trying to please someone who is not a match for me, my product, or my service. As a conscious salesperson, I must accept the truth that someone else is a better match for them. I always do my best to be professional and recommend another company that may better suit the personality or needs of that client. By letting these "energy drains" go, I have freed myself to give other clients exceptional service.

Case in point: In my Millionaire Mindset Program, I offer salespeople, entrepreneurs, and business owners one CD interview a month and articles by other authors on a variety of topics to support their "right thinking." I also offer other business coaches sponsorships to be part of my coaching program to help keep their members motivated. After several successful years with very good word-of-mouth advertising, a particular business coach called wanting to use my coaching program for his members. He wanted to make sure that his people would warm up to me, so I happily spent 90 minutes on a live conference call with him and his membership group. I presented a seminar tailored just for his members and their needs, and I received great feedback from his members and staff. However, I never got even a verbal "thank you" from him. A small red flag went up in my head. That hadn't been my experience with other business coaches I had taken the time and expense to assist.

This prospect then asked if he could have one of my coaching calls for free for his group before he signed a contract. We finally agreed on the terms and set a date. The day before the conference call, one of his staff people called, requesting that I make major changes to the way the conference call would proceed. It took huge expense and effort to pull it off, but we did it. And again, there were no words of appreciation or gratitude.

When it came time to close this client, he made more demands and was generally difficult and critical of my service. Another red flag! He was asking me to break all my own business rules just to make him happy. And the more I did to try to close the sale, the more he would ask for or complain about. And more red flags! He was clearly the kind of person who thought that if he criticized you and your product, you would lower your price to get his business.

After one long, exhausting conversation with him, I realized that if he signed a contract, dealing with him would make my life hell because nothing made him happy! I had had enough stress with him and he simply was not worth it. I looked back over the red flags and assured myself that I had survived before I met him and I would live and thrive after he was gone. I meditated on this for a few days and when I felt clear about what I needed to do, I sent him a letter retracting my offer to do coaching for his group. As you can well imagine, this did not make him happy, but you just can't win them all.

A few months later I found out that listening to my intuition and retreating from his business had been a blessing. I talked to a vendor who dealt with him and was told that this man made a point of bullying people whom he did business with. The poor coach who finally ended up working for him was totally miserable and wished he had never seen the guy and couldn't wait till the agreement came up for renewal to be rid of him!

The lesson here is to honor yourself. When you see really big red flags from a client, be willing to save yourself energy, time, money, and tons of aggravation by letting that client go.

Sell Only Goods and Services You Are Proud to Represent

In my mid-twenties, after several successful sales positions and one year into my career as a commercial real estate agent (in a time of deep recession), I woke up one morning and simply did not want to get out of bed. The cold truth hit me in the face: I hated my sales job. I had lost my motivation. Life was no longer fun. In fact, after a little soul search-ing, I had to admit to myself that I'd only gone into real estate pursuing the big bucks. And unfortunately, not only was I not making the big bucks, but my life was filled with frustration.

What was occurring—though I didn't realize it at the time—was that my belief systems were changing. Up to that point, I had been mov-ing through life determined to establish a lifestyle that I believed meant success—money, titles, and lots of fancy trappings. Clearly, I was at a critical point in my life. I could sell out and continue working in a job that did not bring me happiness, or I could begin to reevaluate and restructure my beliefs about what was really important—money or hap-piness?

Why couldn't I have both? I had been poor and I had been rich, and I can say that money is a handy thing to have if you want to live a com-fortable life. And now I was not bringing in enough to pay my bills for the month. The real estate company loaned me more money than I was making so that, when I did sell something, I already owed it back to them. That meant that I could not quit without owing them money.

Though I felt much pain and confusion at that moment, I heard a small voice inside—the same voice that had led me through other dark moments—telling me to examine the belief systems I was holding on to in my life that were not working. Then I knew I would have to spend time to get clear about my new beliefs and allow them to motivate me toward my next level of success.

So, after many long sleepless nights, I finally began to ask myself some of the most important questions of my life. What did I love to do most? How did I want to live each day? What could I do that would allow me to wake up each morning excited about the day ahead? How could I earn a living and love what I do?

Looking back, I realize it took a great deal of courage to face the reality that my life was not working and to attempt to do something about it. I knew in my heart that whatever I decided, from that point forward I would have to sell only something I totally believed in with all my heart and soul. I was ready to do something that really excited and fulfilled me.

To make a long story short, that is what started me on the path to becoming a speaker and author. Now I sell ideas and training on success-thinking concepts. I can honestly say that I believe in myself and my work one hundred percent. Taking the risk to give up operating my life the way others felt I should and taking control of my own destiny allowed me to truly love what I do. Frankly, because I love what I do, I attract people who want to do business with me. I have never been more successful than I am now, doing what I truly love, in a field in which I have natural capabilities.

Life is way too short to work for an organization that you feel out of integrity with. All too often, we put our own needs on a shelf to serve others' needs and desires. We support others, yet we do not give ourselves permission to pursue our own dreams and desires. Now is the time to look honestly in the mirror and ask, "What do I want? What can I do today to really live my life, not just go through the motions?"

If, as one who aspires to be a conscious salesperson, you feel you cannot sell your current product or service with pride, face it, you are out of integrity with your own truth. You need to do some serious soul searching and ask yourself whether you want to stay where you are or move on to an environment that offers services or products that you feel are in integrity with your truth. Don't discount the pride aspect of representing something; if you don't feel it, you need to keep looking for something that you can feel a sense of honor in representing.

If you work for an organization that does not care about you and its customers, does it serve you to stay there? Get clear about why you are happy or unhappy. The truth will set you free. Remember, destiny is not a matter of chance; it's a matter of choice. That means when you examine your beliefs about what is possible, you acknowledge that you have a valuable contribution and that your talents, skills, and abilities can serve you and your clients.

Let's get even clearer: Unless you are happy with what you are representing, you cannot really serve yourself or others in the highest and best ways. It takes a lot of courage to dare to question what you are selling right now. One of the most spiritual acts you can do is to believe in yourself and listen to your own intuition. Belief in yourself is the one basic, absolutely essential ingredient for anyone who wants to be a conscious salesperson. To believe in yourself, you must know that you stand in integrity with the products or services that you represent.

In my coaching program and speaking engagements over the years I have heard many stories of people staying in jobs they hate. Everyone gets stuck for their own reasons. Many people would rather be unhappy than face the risk of looking or feeling foolish trying to find another job. For some people, the fear of the unknown is just too big for them to conquer.

So, let's touch your own truth to set you free. If right now you are not honest with yourself about how you feel about your current position, what are you waiting for? You may have noticed that your God Source does not offer a neon light in the sky to guide you! Take some time to write out on paper how you feel and what you want. Knowing your own truth will give you the power to fund the necessary changes in your life.

If you have done your self-discovery process and truly don't see a future for yourself where you are, be true to yourself and sincerely start a new position search. Don't wait for life to come to you. God helps those who help themselves. If you do leave your current position for greener pastures, do so with integrity, professionalism, class, and proper notice. Be willing to help train the next person taking your position. Never burn your bridges because you never know when you may need one.

Warning! Don't just be reading these materials and saying to yourself, "She is right; I need to get out of here." All success comes from studying, planning, and then taking action. It's just not bright to quit a job before getting another one. Go to school at night or take online classes; prepare yourself for your future. Become a person who does not have to actively look for a job because your talents, integrity, professionalism, and good personality draw recruiters to try to hire you away from where you are now!

Today is the day to get yourself in a proactive state of mind and start an improvement program on yourself. Just as you would start an exercise program, choose to behave in ways that will assist you in the achievement of your personal and business goals. For more how-tos on programming your mind and motivating yourself, you can read my book *Success Is an Inside Job*, for a fast get-started guide. I share my personal story of how I overcame many odds to achieve.

All Sales Positions Have Imperfections

As Dr. Phil says, "Get real." Don't set yourself up in desire of perfection, because there are no perfect jobs. We will never sell every person we present to, and there may be problems of fulfillment once any sale is made.

Furthermore, there are different personalities everywhere you work and it's not humanly possible for people to agree all the time. In reality, no matter where you work, there will be office politics and difficult people. A conscious salesperson is wise enough to look for the good in people first, and then to focus on the good in people to attract more good to herself.

Acknowledge Your True Nature

Another area where the truth can set you free is accepting yourself as a child of God. You are perfect in the concepts of heaven, though human on earth. We are all on this journey to learn from life and enjoy the process. As a conscious salesperson, accept the truth that your job is to simply offer the best of yourself. Yes, from time to time you will forget to pay attention to the messages of your God Source, as all of us do, but you can easily turn your thoughts to the still, small voice within and resume your path.

Some days, you may be the only person who knows you have stayed in integrity with yourself. You can look yourself in the mirror and know you did the best you could in every way. The only person we ever really need to impress is ourselves. As conscious salespeople, we can know we are honest and filled with integrity because in our hearts we feel it is the right thing to do. And that is enough!

Prayer for Integrity

I bless my sales position because my business is God's business. I offer thoughts of prosperity, abundance, and the best service to everyone I deal with daily. Everything I need is drawn to me though God's sources. Customers, clients, ideas, solutions, and prosperity come to me easily and effortlessly. I bless all my transactions and the people I work with. Love permeates all of my business dealings. My business is God's business and God's divine energy leads me to success. I am in partnership with God; I cannot fail. God is my supply. Amen.

Power Tool Number 6—The Power of Your Imagination

It is said that all that a man achieves and all that he fails to achieve are the direct result of his own thoughts. In his book *University of Success,* Og Mandino says, "All achievements, whether in the business, intellectual, or spiritual world, are the result of definitely directed thought, are governed by the same law and are of the same method. Whatever your present environment may be, you will fall, remain, or rise with your thoughts, your Vision, your Ideal. You will become as small as your controlling desire; as great as your dominant aspiration."

By using your God-given talent to image your sales success in your mind, you add to your capacities of being a conscious salesperson. What you focus on expands. Focus your thoughts on what you want in life; try not to focus on what you do not want in your life. When you use your imagination, or focus, you are envisioning behavioral changes that will show up automatically in your reality.

The images in your mind's eye are very important because images are the language of the brain. As I've said before, taking the time to decide exactly what images you want to go into your personal mind-computer is a powerful tool to aid you in your quest to become a success at sales.

Taking charge of the caliber of information that goes into your subconscious mind allows you to create new references or pictures.

When you are imagining the positive outcomes you want to experience in your life, you will become more enthusiastic about your future. The word "enthusiasm" comes from the Greek "en theos," with a root meaning of "god-inspired." Once you have imagined good things coming to pass in your mind's eye, you feel a sense of eagerness. When you are aflame with enthusiasm, your power expands and your wholehearted involvement becomes contagious. You feel the motivation and inspiration, and you receive the intuition, or guidance, to make your mental rehearsals absolutely real. You literally become a success magnet by attracting people and opportunities to yourself.

I was asked this question by a television interviewer: "Lee, if you could only use one tool for success in sales, what would it be?" I replied without a second's hesitation—the tool of imagination. The old saying "If you can see it, you can do it" is so true. If you can see yourself being successful in sales, then you will have the confidence and direction to aim and use your life energy to make that vision a reality.

Images Are the Language of the Brain

You may never have thought of images being the language of the brain. Since the thoughts that come from our brain influence our future, we want to use our imagination to put into our mind-computers the pictures or references of success. This imagination process is known by many names, such as mental imaging, mental rehearsal, guided imagery, self-hypnosis, and behavior modification. Scientists refer to it as imprinting or modeling.

Please don't be one of those people who let labels keep them from trying something. The truth is, no matter what this tool is called, it is one of the most important tools of the conscious salesperson. Whatever you decide to call your imagination process is okay, but please just do it!

There is nothing mysterious about using your imagination; it is simply a practical, proven application to create a better existence. When you use your imagination you are experiencing your God Source. Your God

Source is the part of you that has a deep sense of knowingness, certainty of power, love, and wisdom.

The best way to prepare for success in life is to imagine yourself being successful. Your imagination is your own personal workshop of the mind. In it, you can see all the possibilities of the future and exactly how to go about creating those dreams. You can rehearse the possibilities, create plans, and visualize ways to succeed, all in the privacy of your mind.

Unless you allow it to be so, your imagination is not bound by limiting beliefs, fears, or past conditioning. Walt Disney said, "If you can dream it, you can do it." Everything we create in the physical world starts as an idea.

Making Your Imagination Work for You

There are the four basic understandings or guidelines you must follow to make your imagination work for you:

1. Desire is the starting point of all creation.
2. I believe that I can manifest my goals.
3. I give myself permission to have what I want.
4. When I have visualized my success, I let go of attachment to the details of how it will arrive at my doorstep, and just listen to my inner guidance as to what I am to do next.

When I was selling electronic equipment to commercial buildings, I always used mental rehearsal before calling on a new client. When I first woke in the morning, I stayed in bed for an extra five minutes and imagined myself at the end of my appointment. I saw myself as confident, knowing all the facts and answering all questions professionally. I then "saw" the end result that I wanted—the client smiling and signing the agreement. I had a strong desire to be a top salesperson. In the evening, just before I went to sleep, I played the same scene over and over in my mind, creating as many details as possible of the sights, sounds, and feelings.

I also did the tangible work of practicing my sales presentation, anticipating possible questions, and having the backup materials needed to satisfy the clients. In other words, I did my homework. My favorite motto is that it is better to be over-rehearsed than ambushed!

When meeting a new potential client I felt confident and comfortable because, in my mind, I had already rehearsed myself getting the sale before we met. I expected to do a great job and I did. As the spiritual masters have said, what you expect in life often becomes your reality. I had a belief that I was going to be successful. I gave myself permission to be good at sales. And last but not least, once I mentally imaged my success I let go and let God handle all the details.

As I realized that the highest use of the mind is to create our reality, these mental imaging tools helped me shape my future as a successful salesperson. This eye-opening concept has guided me since that day, to where I am now a successful and sought-after coach, speaker, and author.

Believe me, I would never have had the confidence to go for my goals in life without mental rehearsal or mental imaging. This tool allowed me to break through barriers of what I could and could not do that I had set up in my own mind. Research shows that the mental practice of making a sales presentation has the same effect as real practice. Using this tool, I worked out kinks in my sales presentations before I got in front of the clients.

Mental imaging can be used in all areas of your life from making a sale to attaining your life's dream goals. All areas of your life can benefit from imagery. It doesn't matter what level your goals are on: physical, emotional, mental, or spiritual.

According to Dr. David Thornburg, who teaches creativity at Stanford's business school, "In mental rehearsal you're engaging your subconscious as an ally in pursuit of goals. With imaging reinforcing the goals' importance, the subconscious will put that goal very high on your priorities, making it far more likely that you'll unconsciously begin adjusting your actions in ways that will make that goal happen for you." The mind is a marvelous tool. When freed, it will find so many ways for us to achieve what we want.

Tap into Your Potential

Sales trainers, counselors, and therapists who recommend mental imaging say it is the true key to tapping into your potential. Their research reveals that all of our skills are learned through the image-making process, whether it's making a sale or dealing with a difficult situation. You use your mind to picture the activity before you actually perform it. Your mind works like a movie projector, screening an endless reel of memories, daydreams, and scenes of situations both real and imagined.

There is more to imagining in the mind than mental rehearsal or suggestion. Our nervous system reacts to mental images in the same way it reacts to images from the external world. In other words, the nervous system cannot tell the difference between an imagined experience and a real experience. Think about the last time you really blew it in a sales call and you felt very embarrassed at your lack of success. Remember all the things that happened and how you felt. The more you think of this situation, the faster your heart beats, your palms start to sweat, and so on. You are reliving the physical dynamics because you have called up the emotions of that painful sales call. It is all recorded in your body's mental computer!

You suffered all the same stress just thinking about the painful sales call because your subconscious mind and your nervous system cannot tell the difference between an imagined situation and the real thing—*ever!* I hope you will stop and think about that fact for a moment because once you truly understand this concept you can stop being tied to your past.

Your present-moment thoughts are your most powerful creative tools. You can create a rich life filled with love, rewarding work, satisfying relationships, health, financial prosperity, inner peace, and harmony. The use of mental imaging gives you a magical tool to tap into the natural goodness and richness of life. Creative mental imaging is magical because it aligns the natural activities of your conscious and subconscious mind with the universal mind that connects all life.

New Views of the Way We Create Our Reality

Over the past century, several courageous Nobel Prize-winning physicists working in prestigious universities received national and global acclaim for their investigations in what is now known as quantum mehcanics. Dr. Niels Bohr, a Nobel laureate in physics (who was at the time considered the most intelligent man in the world, after Einstein), and other international physicists were studying these breakthrough theories that would change the way we see and work within our world. They penetrated the world of subatomic activity and encountered a reality totally different from our classical view of how things function.

These scientists proved that you could co-create the world around you, that how you view physical (external) and mental (internal) reality and your choices and actions in life determine your outcome. The bottom line is, these scientists wanted to prove that your mind's action and external physical objects and occurrences are connected. In other words, our lives are not predetermined before we are born; we have the personal power—and a personal responsibility—to envision what we want.

All this flies in the face of common sense, you might say. So did Newton's theories; so did Einstein's lofty principles. All new breakthrough thinking has to come from the breaking away from old long-held perspectives.

Our Physical Universe Is Made of Energy

We now know that the objects that appear to be solid and separate from each other, in the way our physical senses perceive them, are really made up of moving particles of pure energy. We are all part of a large energy field. All forms of energy are interrelated and can affect one another. Energy vibrates at various rates of speed and light, with differing qualities from very fine to very dense.

Matter is considered to be compact energy and is relatively dense; therefore, it is slower to move and to change. A perfect example would be a rock: even a rock changes over time because of the natural energies of water, light, and wind. On the other hand, our thoughts, which are very light, fine forms of energy, are easy and quick to change. So by using our very malleable and power-filled thoughts, we can affect our outside world.

As I discussed, universal law states that like energies attract. Since energy is magnetic, energy of each certain vibration attracts energy of a similar vibration. Therefore, thoughts and feelings have their own magnetic energy, which also always attracts energy of the same nature.

We are always creating our reality from our thoughts. Our thoughts act like blueprints of the image we want to create. The image magnetizes and guides the physical energy to flow into the form we have imagined and allows us to manifest our desires into reality. Mental imagery is often called the Law of Radiation and Attraction. This is simply the principle that as you sow, so shall you reap, in your thoughts and in your life. We always attract into our lives whatever we strongly believe, think about, or imagine most vividly.

Keep in mind that there are no limits except the limits you put on yourself. You have the power, through your thoughts and imagination, to break through any illusionary barriers holding you back from a prosperous and successful life.

Daydreaming and Fantasizing

Please do not confuse mental imaging with daydreaming or fantasizing. Although both involve the use of your imagination, it's only when you commit yourself to a goal that you can truly take advantage of mental imaging. Daydreams and fantasies are usually unrealistic thoughts that we don't expect to actually happen or have little investment in, such as finding a magic bottle with a genie who pops out and drops millions of dollars in your lap. Daydreaming or mere undirected wishful thinking does not have the power to release the latent forces within you to bring about these fantasies.

It's important to point out that mental imaging is not a method of self-deception; it is one of the strongest tools known to date for self-direction and tapping into your potential. By becoming the star, director, editor, and writer of the movie of your life, you are synthesizing the experience of your success in your mind and allowing your body to start vibrating at a new level of attraction. The vision acts like a magnet; once the image is fixed in the mind, your subconscious is alerted to bring about factors that will help you achieve the goal you just programmed. In time, our deliberate visions become self-fulfilling. This mental training is simply a way of reprogramming the mind to achieve more positive behaviors, feelings, and results, and to see new opportunities.

Movies of the Mind

You have the ability to create movies in your mind and you do it with total perfection. You do it every time you think of someone or remember something or even daydream. Without being aware of it, you create pictures in your mind in countless different situations every day. For example, look at an object near you; examine it in detail and note its shape, color, and size. After you have examined it, close your eyes and picture in your mind what you just saw. If you can do that, you've just proved to yourself how you can direct your imagination.

How each of us uses our inner movie screen differs slightly. Some people see their picture in color, while others see it in black and white. I am happy to report that you cannot do it wrong because there is no right or wrong way. However you sense and feel your images is just perfect for you. The more you practice using mental imaging, the better your brain can become at directing what happens in your daily life. This allows you to be more in control of your experiences.

By using mental imaging, we can create a state of awareness in which we are not using logical, linear, or analytical thinking, but instead we are actually experiencing through feeling. We live in a world of rationality and often we forget our intuitive, creative selves. We have to accept ourselves as the cause or creator of our lives. We must rediscover ourselves as the cause rather than the effect of the quality of our lives. Our inner experience is so directly connected to our outer experiences that we can affect our moment-to-moment living. By using mental imaging you can create an entirely new dimension of success to your life and work.

Easy Steps for Using Your Imagination

The best way to begin using the power of imagination is to first get your body into the correct mode for programming. This correct mode is to be deeply relaxed in both body and mind. It's only when you are relaxed that your mind will open to fresh ideas and new techniques. When your mind and body are deeply relaxed, your brain actually becomes slower. This slower state is known as the alpha state.

Two of the most effective times to use your imagination to achieve your goals are as you wake up in the morning, while your mind and body are very relaxed and receptive, and last thing at night just before sleeping. Research in this area has found that by using your imagination during this relaxed time, your subconscious records new programs more effectively. Experts on creative visualizing agree that when your spine is straight you come into the alpha state faster.

The second step for effective mental imaging is having a clearly defined goal that you would like to achieve or create in your life. You must have the faith and belief that you can realize your goal. Remember, the details of how your goal comes to you may not be yours to handle, so simply believe that you can have or do it!

The third step is to create a mental picture as if the goal were already yours; act as if the picture were real today, not some time in the future. Be sure to fill in the small details of the sights, colors, smell, textures, and feelings; the more realistic the details, the better. If you can see, hear, touch, smell, and taste your goal, your mental picture will be that much clearer and will attract like energies better.

Imagine only that you have achieved your desire. Do not reinforce negative pictures, should any arise for you. It's very important to see only what you want so that you imprint the correct new pictures in your subconscious mind.

The fourth step is to focus on your mental picture as often as possible. For 21 days, envision your success in great detail at least twice a day, for five to ten minutes each time. Research has proven that it takes a minimum of three weeks for an old mental image to dissolve and a new mental image to form.

In addition, several times a day you should stop and take about 16 seconds to envision exactly what you want. It only takes about 16 seconds to link up vibrationally to whatever you are focusing on. Yes, I know that sounds like a short amount of time but, once you have carefully created the desired image in your mind in those longer sessions, you can return to it more easily and quickly focus your mental energy on it. That's enough to set your mental vibrations on the same frequency as your goal, attracting people and events whose vibrations are similar to your own.

Another advantage of frequently envisioning your desired goals is that it can be a form of renewal of purpose and attitude. Think about it: Renewal means to restore or refresh your view, rejuvenate your approach, and reestablish your focus. Since the body follows the mind, when you spend a moment seeing yourself in a happy, peaceful environment, you automatically feel that way. And who doesn't need that in the middle of a tough workday?

The fifth step is to provide yourself with a tangible picture of or a representative object for the goals you are consciously creating. Start to collect the symbols for what you want to create in your life from various sources, such as magazines or newspapers. These symbols can be in the form of pictures, sayings, or statements that represent the goals and dreams in your life. Put your reminders in places where you will see them several times every day to reinforce your true wants and desires. Perhaps you'd like to select an object that represents the goal to you, such as a big brass key to represent that new home you want to attract, and that you can use as a paperweight.

The sixth step is to always be in a good state of mind when you envision what you want. Dr. Maltz, in his famous book *Psycho-Cybernetics*, repeatedly says you must relax and unwind prior to going into the theater of your mind. Once you relax and find a good feeling place within you, then put feeling and deep emotion into the process of imaging what you want. He suggested an image to think about. Imagine letting all the negative stress out of the body like a large valve on a tire letting out air. This image helps you get into an altered state where your mind is easily accepting the "new you." The reason is, of course, that your subconscious mind is influenced through emotion more than any other factor. Vivid images that are not mixed with positive feel-good emotions won't lead to positive change.

Esther and Jerry Hicks, the authors of *Ask and It Is Given*, say:

Remember, you live in a Vibration Universe, and all things are managed by the law of attraction. And you get what you think about, whether you want it or not, because whenever you achieve vibration harmony with something because you are giving it your attention, the vibration essence of it will, in some way, begin to show up in your life experience.

So, you could say that the universe responds to your vibration offerings, to your point of attraction, to the thoughts you think, and the way you feel. The universe is not responding to what has been manifested in your experience, but instead, to the vibration that you are now offering. The universe makes no distinction between your actually having a million dollars and your giving thought to having a million dollars. Your point of attraction is about your thoughts, not about your manifestations.

Be a Visionary for Your Own Future

Shakespeare said, "Assume a virtue if you have it not." One of the secrets of success is to not work so hard with your physical sweat; instead, use your mind to work out the details of how to be the person you want to be. The difference between average people and outstanding people is the degree of motivation within them. Are you motivated to spend ten minutes a day envisioning the future you want to create for yourself? By deliberately imaging the experience of success in your mind, you can turn aspirations into realities. Thomas Edison once said, "Good fortune is what happens when opportunity meets with planning." Prepare yourself for success!

Where Two or More Are Gathered

One of the best kept secrets of successful salespeople who have accelerated their careers and personal life is to belong to a Mastermind group. In Matthew 18:20 of the Bible we read, "For where two or three are gathered together in my name, there am I in the midst of them."

There is an exponential factor that applies when people gather with one intention in their minds and hearts. The unity of their purpose creates a growth environment as their consciousness expands towards the recognition of God at work in their lives. It is scientifically proven that people who consistently work with other like-minded people come up with more creative solutions and better ideas and seem to enjoy life more.

A Mastermind group consists of like-minded people who come together on a regular basis to share information, ideas, suggestions, and resources. Often a Mastermind group will help to hold the vision of each other's goals using the mental imaging process. Some groups agree to pray for each other's success in achieving personal or professional goals. These activities increase the vibrational attraction of each group member's goals.

Being a member of a Mastermind group will help you advance your own goals and bring you solutions that would have taken you much longer to achieve on your own. Other people's knowledge, experience, and perspective will take you beyond your own view of life.

In a Mastermind group, participants are encouraged to expand their mindsets to new heights of creative thinking and to get the feedback of others who are not emotionally attached to an outcome. As Jack Canfield said in his book *The Success Principles*, "Mastermind, therefore, is both the power that comes to us from each other and the power that comes to us from above."

As a professional coach, I have had the opportunity to run several Mastermind groups. In my groups I have noticed that the Mastermind members start to think outside of their normal perceptions because of the suggestions and points of view of other members. I have also experienced that bonds form within the groups with a sincere desire to assist each member to reach their goals. Everyone who sincerely commits to meeting with other like-minded people in a Mastermind environment will find solutions they never could have seen without the guidance of the group and they will see a dramatic increase in their business.

As a conscious salesperson you are probably involved in sales meetings with your own company. Those meetings can be powerful if you go into them with an attitude of open-mindedness. The purpose of these meetings is to give you support, motivation, and inspiration to become a better salesperson and to offer better service to your clients. Since each person in a sales meeting is either part of the problem or part of the solution, speak up and contribute to the meetings by sharing things you have learned from seminars, books, and other salespeople. One of the greatest things you can do for others is share information. What you sow is what you reap.

The author Napoleon Hill often said that brains are like batteries. The more batteries you have the more power you produce, and the same goes with brains. If you are serious about being outstanding in your field, it would benefit you a great deal to join a Mastermind group.

Prayer to Enhance Imagination

Dear God,

Assist me today to delicately guide my thoughts and images in my mind's eye to those of peace, harmony, perfect health, happiness, prosperity, and well-being in my life. Allow me to see myself as confident, filled with vitality and good health, enthusiastic about my life and work. Allow me to work out any "problems" in my mind and to see the perfect solutions as they come to me. Thank you for your guidance. Amen.

Power Tool Number 7—The Power of a Prosperity Consciousness

Money is simply a symbol of energy.

How many times have you thought to yourself, if I only had more money, all my problems would be solved? In truth, money usually has very little to do with your level of personal happiness. In and of itself, money possesses no value. As Tony Robbins used to say, "Money is just small green paper with dead notables on it." It's not the money! It's how you use it that determines its true worth.

Pay close attention: It is very important to realize money for what it really is, which is just a tool, no more and no less. Money is simply a symbol of energy. Just as your lights turn on when you hit the electric switch, just as your car gets you from one location to another, money is simply a financial tool that, when used correctly, can assist you in reaching your goals.

In his book *The Trick to Money Is Having Some!* Stuart Wilde says, "Abundance will never be a factor of how much money one has. Rather, it is always a factor of how one feels about what money one does have."

Let's begin by defining wealth. It is not just money, because having more money alone will not always bring you happiness. Wealth is being at peace with yourself and feeling fulfilled in what you do. It is enjoying and appreciating your life, your family, and your career. Money is only one form of abundance. There are many forms of abundance in our lives: love, happiness, friendship, good health, vitality, and joy.

Everyone is interconnected by one energy source. Jung called it the collective unconscious. Still others call it spirit or the grace of God. Whatever name you use, the connection is there. Prosperity means integration with the God Source in all things. The God Source is unlimited, so everything is unlimited. If everything is unlimited, so are wealth and prosperity in your life.

Catherine Ponder, who has written many books on prosperity, says that "prosperity is more than money, wealth, and financial security; it is the way you live your life and the way you focus your life energy; it is the balance of what you can and cannot control; it is loving yourself and others; it is counting your blessings and enjoying who and what you currently are now." The definition of the word "prosper" is to flourish, succeed, and thrive, to experience favorable results and to get what you want out of life. It is more than wealth and financial security.

In this chapter I want to share with you the need for something called "prosperity consciousness" in your life. Increasing the level of awareness about your ability to create prosperity enables you to create more self-confidence, self-trust, and self-esteem. These new empowering traits will help you generate and create wealth and financial security in the sales field.

Ralph Waldo Emerson described prosperity as the law of compensation whereby like attracts like, meaning that what you radiate out in your thoughts, feelings, mental pictures, and words, you also attract into your life. Your beliefs about money will determine how you relate to it and how you spend it. If you see the world as having unlimited resources, which it does, then you tend to feel more relaxed about money. You know you can earn it, or attract it, whenever you need it if you're willing to do whatever it takes.

Conversely, if you think you can only receive money by working extremely hard, through toil and sweat, then that is exactly what you'll end up doing. Why not make life a little easier for yourself? Why exhaust yourself with so much toil and sweat when you could apply your mental capacities to achieve even more?

Great spiritual teachers have taught us over history that we can learn to create our destiny through our thoughts. We can use our thought energy rather than physical effort to produce results that go beyond anything we will be able to create with just physical effort alone.

My sincere desire is to share with you strategies to empower you and to help you gain the confidence that comes from understanding how to create the life you want. It is my goal to give you the tools to create your dreams, hopes, and fantasies. You can learn to take responsibility for your life, to enjoy personal and professional growth. These tools can help you to achieve new levels of clarity about your dreams and goals and to be in control of your own life.

As a conscious salesperson, you must open your mind to the perspective that creating wealth and abundance has a lot to do with internal decisions and external knowledge, and little to do with the state of the national economy. We must rise above the popular belief that it is necessary to be affected by the economy. Abundance is a mindset, not an external condition that controls your destiny. God has filled the Earth with good things for us to enjoy and use. You can claim the abundance you so richly deserve because there are no limits to what we can create with these unlimited resources around us.

You Must Be Responsible for Your Wealth

You must start to take action to create whatever you want out of life. Be kind to yourself, and allow yourself to build your confidence by simply taking small steps in the direction of your goals. Try something new every single day. It's very interesting to note that changing just a few small actions or habits in your life will compound itself. In a few months, these changes can produce dramatic results in professional and personal life.

Most of us did not grow up with an educational system that taught us about how to create prosperity or abundance. Unless you have deliberately sought out books, tapes, seminars, or been fortunate enough to have had mentors in your life who have shared this valuable information with you, you have been on your own.

You may have thought that just being lucky, or working hard, or investing wisely would create wealth. Those things certainly can assist you in becoming more prosperous. However, there is a little-known secret about how to create success. The secret is that you must focus on what you want to occur in your life instead of what you don't want to occur. Whatever you focus on is what you will get—energy follows thought. Pay attention to this one, folks! The more you focus on being poor, the poorer you will become. The more you focus on and picture and talk about abundance, the more you will do to get it. Further, by keeping your mind filled with thoughts of abundance, more elements of abundance will be attracted to you.

To attract great prosperity into your life you must pay attention to the quality of information you put into your computer, your brain. It truly is your success mechanism. For a strong prosperity consciousness, pay even closer attention to your self-talk, because it is your self-talk that guides you to live in poverty consciousness or prosperity consciousness. The decision is up to you. Your success depends on the caliber of information you allow in your environment.

In sales, your success will depend on your self-talk as well as your spoken word. You must be aware of what you are saying to yourself and others. You must also replace those thoughts that do not serve you. Instead of saying, "I don't have enough money," replace that with, "I have an abundance of money." Our positive thoughts are more powerful than our negative ones, so remember that you can reprogram your mind-computer with your thoughts. Use the supporting statements called affirmations. They can help you create your own destiny since you are the controller of your wealth through your thoughts.

Obviously your intention is to create abundance and the prosperity to obtain the things you want in your life. By using affirmations you will actually be reprogramming your subconscious mind to accept these new thoughts as reality. As you imprint this information on your mind, it begins to create changes in your life to match this new inner reality.

Your goal is to focus on the new reality you want to create for yourself. Take on the spirit of creating something new, rather than changing or resisting what is now. You do have the power to co-create with God and create a new destiny for yourself by giving yourself permission to go for what you want. Whatever we think about ourselves and our abilities on a consistent basis will determine how successful and prosperous we become.

Here are some examples of affirmations that you can use to feel more prosperous. Add new ones that feel comfortable to you. Try to use your affirmations many times per day with as much emotion as possible to imprint them on your mind-computer. For example, say them first thing in the morning and just before you make a sales call. As you are going from one sales appointment to the next, turn off your radio and simply say your affirmations with as much gusto as possible. Notice how good you feel when you walk into that next appointment. They will feel your good vibrations! Hey, don't take my word for it about the power of this technique—just give it a try.

Prosperity Thoughts

I am in this world to experience and enjoy success.
I have every natural right to be wealthy and successful.
I am confident of my talent to create success.
I am enthusiastic and confident.
I choose to be prosperous.
I love myself more and more daily.
I have the energy, resources, and time to be successful and prosperous.
I am more intelligent every day, in every way.
I think of new creative ways to attract money.
I am powerful and confident and that attracts to me the right people and the right situations.
I am willing to be powerful and successful.
I have valuable contributions.
I reinforce my successes as I correct my errors.

Enjoy Your Successes

If we really face life and look back on what we have been able to accomplish in the past, we are already successful. You already have knowledge, experience, people who love you, and the freedom to make choices that serve you. It's time for you to recognize your own unlimited opportunities. Start to catch yourself doing things right and congratulate yourself often. Begin to appreciate yourself and count your blessings.

Isn't it interesting how most people look ahead to the next mountain peak in life, without ever taking the time to appreciate the heights they just conquered? Salespeople are famous for only enjoying their sales successes for a few minutes. When you have a successful day you should celebrate! Get into the habit of celebrating life whenever possible. When you celebrate your successes you are training your subconscious mind to create more awareness of your success, which will help aim you in those directions. In support of the joy of success, your intuition will kick in and tell you to call on a certain client, perhaps assisting you to make sales you would not have made.

Also, be sure to look at the small things in your life that give you pleasure, like a sunset, a great meal, playing with your children, or reading a good book. That is the true wealth in your life.

By appreciating and acknowledging your successes, not only will you enjoy them more, but you will have more energy and confidence to create even more success, abundance, and prosperity for your future. All of our energy will create some type of result. If we focus on remembering the feelings of mastery in the various areas of our lives, those feelings will actually imprint on our mind-computer and help us create success for the future. Remember, your thoughts create your beliefs, and your beliefs create your reality.

Sales Success Evidence Book

To assist you on your journey as conscious salespeople, it is important to track your successes and acknowledge your efforts in achieving goals. I suggest that you create a "Sales Success Evidence Book." The book is a tool to help you feel in control and powerful in your life. For this fun project, invest in a large, inexpensive photo album and fill it with all your past successes, such as pictures, awards, articles about yourself, letters of congratulation, sales contest mementoes, and graphic charts of your top sales records. This is not a brag book to show to other people; it is a tool that is only for you. Let it remind you just how successful you really are.

I have found that salespeople who review their successes before they go out to make sales calls tend to have more sales that day. You are tuning your mind-computer to vibrational harmony with successful selling. You might want to review your book every morning before you start making sales calls to reinforce your beliefs that you have the skills, talent, knowledge, and persistence to be successful in your sales. When you take just three to five minutes a day to remember how great you felt when you met your goals, you guarantee that, no matter what challenges come your way, you have the resources to handle it. After all, the evidence is right there before you in your Evidence Book!

I have personally used this confidence-boosting technique for many years. Even today, when I have a bad day or I have made a mistake or failed at something, I take the time to go back over my Evidence Books. I have them lined up in my personal office, so that any time I need a boost, I can easily pull them out and acknowledge my hard work, my devotion, and my tenacity. There is nothing that can give you more motivation than acknowledging the success you've already enjoyed.

As a side note, since you are the role models for your children, you might want to start a different kind of evidence book called a Victory Book for each of your children. Every time they get a good report card or do something that they are proud of, please take the time to record that achievement in your child's book. This is a wonderful way to boost their confidence. Next time your child comes home fearful about not being able to do something, you can pull out their Victory Book and remind them how they were successful in the past.

If you are a sales manager, you should have all of your salespeople create one of these powerful tools to review every workday morning to help them create a high level of confidence before they start their day. This one tool will build self-confidence for anyone in the sales world. Remember, what you focus on expands.

PreViewing: A Spiritual Exercise in Creating Your Future

The next exercise I suggest to help you take your sales career to an entirely new level is called PreViewing. It is a form of writing affirmations and goals in a story format. This is one of the most compelling and successful processes I have ever experienced.

This technique is actually a form of prayer. As a conscious salesperson, your goal is to connect your spiritual nature with your daily sales work to create prosperity, and PreViewing is one of the most powerful ways to do it. Any message you regularly give your subconscious mind will imprint and start to become part of your comfort zone. These messages become part of your perceptions of yourself. Since you are a self-fulfilling prophecy, it behooves you to do as many things as possible to create a prosperous new personal image of yourself as a conscious salesperson who has partnered with God.

PreViewing is easy and can be done anywhere and any time that you have a few minutes to sit down and write out your vision of your desires for your future. You are the star, director, and producer of this story. If you give yourself permission to be true to yourself and honestly write down exactly how you would like to see your life unfold, this process can be exciting and productive. Also write down ways that you assist and empower others. Experiment and have fun with PreViewing for just 30 days. You will be amazed at the miracles that happen for you and for others in your life.

Your true goal in PreViewing is to *feel* as you want to feel. As you write and visualize your desires, you create vibrational harmony by experiencing the thoughts and feelings associated with the achievement of your goals. The true secret power for manifesting your perfect life is to be able to feel as if you already have the qualities you want or the object you desire. Feelings are vibrational thoughts and are governed by universal law, which asserts that like energies attract. When you can create the internal imagery of feeling prosperous, you can attract the physical equivalent of being prosperous.

Most people spend their lives observing conditions and reacting to circumstances. Let go of this old belief and step into your role as co-creator with the God Source. Be proactive and co-create! Boost your faith in yourself and the God Source. There are no limitations except the ones you put on yourself. My experience is a constant reminder that through God I can do anything. God is my source and my supply.

When scripting your life desires, it's important to be as general in your word pictures as possible, but state enough to get a good feeling. You can become more specific as time goes on, and by then you will have developed your skill using this process.

In this process you are giving your subconscious the clear message that this is the direction in which you want to aim your life energy. You are letting your God Source know you are asking for help to pursue this direction. Be very clear about the fact that God has a much bigger staff working on this than you do and can arrange details and circumstances much better than you can.

This information about PreViewing was in one of my educational videos, *Take Control of Your Life*. A salesman from New York bought my video at one of my seminars and he wrote to me four months after viewing it to say:

> I have been a professional hard-core salesman from the old school for about 27 years, and I am blown away with the power and impact of this technique you shared called PreViewing. In truth the only reason I tried it was because I was nearly desperate. Things were not going well for me. I could not understand what was going on. I was losing sales and customers daily. I was angry and frustrated. I was taking my hostility out on everyone, my family, customers, and my co-workers. My sales manger and I were at it tooth and nail. She gave me one month to pull myself together or I was out!
>
> I started PreViewing, as you suggested, and it felt weird at first. I felt like a liar to be saying all these good things about myself that were not true. But I kept writing. After about four pages of PreViewing my future, I felt a shift in my attitude. I realized that maybe my attitude was part of my problem. I started thinking about how lucky and blessed I was with my sales job. I felt much better that day. I now get up every morn-

ing and script. I can sum it up in one word. Miracles!! I have seen my life turn around since I focused on what I wanted and asked God for help. My sales are up again. My relationships are the best with my customers and I feel younger and more alive. This is one process I will now do forever. As you say, the inter nal work is more important than the external! Well, I am a true believer now. Thank you.

—T. L. Redmond

As you read this book and decide to start the exercises, I suggest that you take small, simple steps. Be kind to yourself and build your confidence by patiently taking small steps in the direction of your goals. Try something new every single day. As I mentioned earlier, it's very interesting to note that changing just a few small actions or habits in your life will compound itself. In a few months, these changes can produce dramatic results in your professional and personal life.

It's important to have this open dialogue with your God Source. Why not make life a little easier on yourself? Why exhaust yourself, when you can apply your spiritual capacities and achieve even more through God? I would like to share with you a prosperity prayer that I have used for years. I say it out loud at least once a day.

Prayer for a Prosperous Consciousness

God's wealth is circulating in my life now.
God's wealth flows to me in avalanches of abundance.
All my needs, desires, and goals are met instantaneously.
I am one with God and God is everything.
Everything I want and need comes to me now through God's laws of action.
So be it.

Power Tool Number 8—
The Power of Intuition

A Strong
Feeling

Sixth
Sense

In my
Heart

Gut
Feeling

A Hunch

Instinct

Listening
to God

All of these terms describe the same thing: Intuition. We just use different names according to our environment. Our intuition is our inner voice and inner knowing. Our personal intuition provides us with information that we have no logical way of knowing. Usually, this is information which, if we act upon it, can be useful, and helpful in our sales career, as well as in our spiritual growth. You can use your intuition to turn problems into opportunities.

Intuition, listening to that inner part of yourself, is clearly one of the most important areas for personal development if you are interested in sales success, prosperity, and peace of mind. There are various ways in which we can hear God or receive intuitive information. Your intuitive insights come to you as sudden breakthrough thoughts, revelations, or urges. These revealing flashes of useful information can help you make better choices about your sales directions and financial decisions, and help you to be a better manager or parent. It's a natural human function and your closest advisor.

Albert Einstein said, "The mind can only proceed so far on what it knows and can prove. There comes a point where the mind takes a leap—call it intuition or what you will—and comes out on a higher plane of knowledge."

If you think about it, most of your current knowledge has been taught to you by the society in which you live, and much of that is outdated and obsolete. Logic and analysis can lead you only halfway to a good decision. The next step frequently requires using your intuitive powers. Pay attention to and rely on that internal part of yourself, that voice inside that tells you when things *feel* right. Within you are resources that you may not have discovered. Listen to your own heart and do what feels right to you.

As we discussed earlier, the subconscious mind remembers everything it has ever heard, read, seen, or been exposed to by your senses. It's an enormous memory bank that will respond to your every request. When you ask it questions, your subconscious mind goes into a search mode, seeking the information to supply your conscious mind with the best answer. The intuitive faculty of your mind-body analyzes all the available data—including some that your conscious mind is not aware of—and makes a decision that's just right for you. It does this all in one step, without your conscious mind's help. In fact, many times your learned knowledge gets in the way of making a good decision! You must listen to that inner wisdom before making decisions if you want your life to be more rewarding and easier.

Case in point: After being in sales for a few years, I had saved some money and needed to invest it. One of my clients recommended a good investment advisor. I went to see this advisor, whose expensive office was downtown in the most prestigious office building. He told me how successful he was at making his clients rich. Yet, something did not feel right to me. The longer I sat in his office the more uncomfortable I became. I actually started to feel sick to my stomach and my body felt like it was shaking. I knew I had to get out of this guy's office. I left his office feeling depressed and out of sorts. I never went back to see him again because something about him was just not right to me, though with my logical mind I could not figure out what was wrong.

I didn't think of this investment advisor again until about six months later, when his picture was on the front page of our local newspaper. He was accused of defrauding people out of their life savings. This experience was a very big wake-up call to me, and since then I have always paid attention to the way I *feel* around people and I honor those feelings regardless of what appears to be reality. My intuition has proven time and time again that it is one of the few things I can trust in life.

It is interesting that in our western culture, we seek to understand almost all of our experiences through logical, linear, analytical thinking processes. We use words to communicate this kind of thinking. Because words are our way of understanding our world, we've almost forgotten that we also have an intuitive, creative nature. We have been programmed by society to be so logical and analytical in our thinking that we forget our intuitive abilities. We're not trained to say "I feel" but rather "I think." If we deny and cut off our intuition, we get trapped by concepts learned only through our culture-programmed minds. Yesterday's learned beliefs cannot solve today's challenges nor help us capitalize on tomorrow's opportunities.

In our culture we have been conditioned to believe that if you can not relate to something with your five senses—that is, to see, touch, taste, hear, or smell it—then "it" does not exist. Our educational system only values rote memorization and analytical processes of thinking and does not value intuitive thinking. Our school systems give very little attention or support to those students displaying creative or artistic talents, which are usually thought of as based on the intuitive processes of the mind. So it's no surprise that we're afraid to trust that those thoughts or feelings which sometimes just "come to us" have valuable and useable information.

Only by learning to trust that inner knowledge and intuition can you really achieve your true potential, both in life and in your sales career. Our lifestyle and the demands of our careers have accelerated, and often we don't have time to gather appropriate information before making a decision. We must learn to seize the moment and listen to our inner wisdom.

Ernest Holmes, in his book *The Science of Mind*, says:

> There are three ways by which we gather knowledge: through science, through opinion, and through intuition or illumination. These channels represent spiritual capacities since each is an avenue leading to self-knowledgeness, and self-knowingness is the very nature and essence of Spirit. Science is Spirit inducing its own laws. Intuition is Spirit knowing itself. . . . We should think of our spirit as being some part of the Universal Spirit, and of our minds as open to the Divine. As any specific knowledge must come from the center of all knowledge, it follows that whenever and wherever the mind of man is open to the Divine, it will receive instruction and direction from the center and source of All. Science, invention, art, literature, philosophy and religion have one common center from which, through experience, is drawn all knowledge.

As a conscious salesperson, realize that making decisions about your daily life, as well as your major career moves, requires both the culture-driven, logical left side of your brain and the intuitive, creative right side of your brain. You must achieve integration of your analytical and intuitive thinking. You can think of this whole-brain integration as thinking with one foot on earth and one foot in heaven.

Today, many people are afraid to listen to and trust their intuition, but if you look at history, it has been taught by all the great spiritual teachers of mankind: listen to the inner guide, the still, small voice. All answers are within your own self.

I have lived my life with great success by using my intuition, doing what I feel I should do versus what my brain or other people told me was the right thing to do. I have painfully learned that if I do not listen to my inner voice, I nearly always regret my actions.

Have you ever had a feeling that you should call on a particular client? Then, after you ignored your inner nudging, later found out that, had you just called on that client, you would have made the sale? How many times have you had a feeling that it was going to be a waste of time to call on a certain client, but you made the call anyway and the client was not even in the building? As a conscious salesperson, you must develop and use these natural abilities—your intuition—to be successful in the sales world.

One of my clients, who is a top salesperson in the printing business, told me a story about how, at the end of a very long day, as she was driving back from her last appointment she decided not to go back to the office but to just go home. Just before she reached the street she normally took to go to the office, though, she had an intuitive hunch that she should go there. She tried to talk herself out of the feeling, but it was so strong that she finally gave in and went back to the office.

She said she had barely unlocked the door when the phone rang. It was a prospect that she had been pursuing for about two years! She was surprised when she heard the caller say, "Our company just landed a huge international account and we need a huge printing job done as soon as possible." As she was writing down his needs he said to her, "This is your lucky day because if you had not been there tonight to get this started, I would have had to call on one of your competitors to get this project done, since I am leaving tomorrow to meet this new client in London to sign the agreement."

This sale turned out to be the largest-volume sale of her career! If she had not listened to her inner urges, she would have missed it entirely. She told me later that this account alone allowed her to pay for her son's entire college education. This client consistently did so much business with her each month that she was almost always the top producer of her office. She said she would never doubt her intuition again!

In truth, all of us get these intuitive flashes, but we don't all have confidence in this type of insight. I suggest you have some fun in life and start testing your intuitive abilities. For the next 30 days, when your phone rings, ask yourself who it is before you answer; count up how many times you're right. Using caller ID does not count!

Since I travel a great deal, I play one of my favorite games while waiting for an elevator. I try to guess which one will come first; I am right much of the time. There are dozens of small games you can play with yourself to strengthen your abilities. Your intuitive "muscle" gets stronger as you use it, which will increase your percentage of accurate information. The purpose of these games is to build confidence so that when you really need your intuition, you will trust and listen to it.

Ours is a world where science has succeeded in explaining most observable phenomena, which makes it hard for us to accept as real anything that has not been explained by scientific study. Most people have lost their abilities to "hear" their intuition simply because they don't use this natural faculty and, as we all know, when you don't use something, you lose it. How many times have you personally experienced an instance of mental telepathy and considered it just a coincidence?

Physicists and psychologists say there is evidence of an energy link between everything in the universe. Everything that happens is simultaneously encoded in this energy pattern. This concept makes telepathic and clairvoyant abilities seem natural and more plausible, and gives us a deeper understanding of how intuition works. In Eastern philosophy, it is believed that each mind has access to the whole of a universal intellectual pattern.

Intuition has been called a mystical power, a guardian angel that takes care of us. Many spiritual teachers have validated the fact that you can gain knowledge without rational thought and that it comes from some awareness just below the conscious level.

In his book *Psycho-Cybernetics*, Dr. Maxwell Maltz writes, "You must learn to trust your creative mechanism to do its work and not jam it by becoming too concerned or too anxious as to whether it will work or not, or by attempting to force it by too much conscious effort. You must let it work, rather than make it work."

Trusting yourself is an important part of learning to use intuition.

You'll find that certain activities or surroundings can be very conducive to intuition. Experiment and find out what works best for you. The most important fundamentals are to allow the mind to be receptive to different ideas and to have faith in your own abilities.

Please understand that I am not suggesting that you shouldn't do your homework when you make decisions. It's important to do the research to support your feelings. What I am suggesting is that you also ask for guidance, then listen to your hunches and, only then, make your decision. Listening to your intuition is just adding another resource to your existing toolbox of life strategies.

In *Personal Power through Awareness*, Sanaya Roman writes, "Intuition talks to you in present time. Through urges, flashes of ideas, insights, and feelings, intuition moves you in certain directions. To hear it, pay attention to your inner world of ideas and feelings. If you are forcing yourself to do one thing while your feelings are urging you to do something else, you are not paying attention to your intuition. Your intuition sends you messages constantly, telling you every moment what to do to open your energy. It is always directing you towards aliveness and a higher path."

One of the best tips I can share with you for making a decision about almost anything is to notice whether it feels right. When things seem to fall into place easily, people are cooperative, and you have a very positive feeling, it usually means you are on the right track. Monitor your feelings. If you feel unsure about your decision, you feel anxious and nervous, if you experience tightness in your body, then maybe you should postpone your decision until these uneasy feelings go away or you've gathered more information. It's wise not to make a decision when you are not *feeling right* about an action or decision.

It's very important to access your emotions. Keep yourself centered to feel in control, and do what you believe in. Keep in mind that your intuition has a proven track record (if you have developed it) and your conscious mind can mislead you if given the wrong information to make a decision.

Your Clients Have Intuition, Too

Imagine this: You are on a sales call and you are giving your prospects logical and intellectual reasons why they should buy your product. But deep down, hidden away, you are feeling unsure of yourself. You have fears that your supplier cannot deliver on time or you don't feel worthy of a large commission, or maybe you dislike your prospect. All those feelings are energy that's being transmitted by you, and your prospects may be picking up on your subtle energy patterns or thoughts, intellectually or subliminally.

Your inner thoughts and feelings are just as important as your physical sales presentation because your inner thoughts affect your prospect's decisions. As a conscious salesperson, you must be aware of the feelings you are experiencing because others can pick up your energy transmissions. Keep in mind that when clients spend money, they want to feel safe to buy things. Just like you, they can sense danger or safety on conscious and unconscious levels. Human beings just seem to be "wired" to intuitively pick up fear, danger, or lack.

Learning to Trust Your Own Intuition

As a conscious salesperson you want to develop your abilities to hear and trust your intuition. Here are some suggestions to help you increase your awareness of your inner voice. Keep in mind that when you are feeling pressured or stressed you will not have a clear channel to hear your inner wisdom.

1. Get into a receptive state: calm your breathing and detach your thoughts from the outer world of people, things, and activities; turn your mind inward upon itself. Do your best to shut out all the material cares, problems, and worries of the day, and allow yourself to feel a sense of connection with your God Source. Once you are in this calm state of mind, pray and ask for answers. Have faith that you can tap into your own natural ability, your own intuition. Know that, in this activity, you are connected to your God Source.

2. To stimulate new and creative thoughts, do things differently by changing your daily routines. Instead of listening to the news or reading the paper in the morning, try meditating and see how that affects your level of intuition.

3. Your body is the instrument of your intuition, so it's important to be aware of your body and start to listen to it. There is a logical reason why we call intuition a "gut" feeling or a hunch. The solar plexus is a large network of nerves located behind the stomach. It is said to be the seat of our emotions. This nerve plexus can give you an accurate, gut-level reaction to people, new ideas, or situations.

4. When troubled by a problem or a situation that you need guidance about, allow yourself to redefine the problem frequently. Writing out the problem gives you the opportunity to determine how you really view it.

5. Get different perspectives on your problem by asking several trusted individuals for their thoughts. You may not take their advice or agree with them, but it does open your mind to a new way of looking at the problem. Often, opening your mind to consider several alternatives simultaneously leads to an appropriate solution. Be flexible. Get out of your boxed-in thinking and consider the issue from a new perspective.

6. You don't have to be sitting in your office to come up with creative and intuitive solutions! Allow yourself to play, take a walk, or just enjoy nature. Play hooky for an hour and then come back to work on the problem.

7. Adopt a childlike view of the situation. Children often see the obvious where adults make things harder and more complicated than necessary.

8. When trying to get information from your intuition, pay attention to

your dreams and your daydreams; they are your personal, nonverbal imagery. Keep in mind that images are the language of the brain. You might have a dream that answers your needs if you are paying attention.

9. Do not feel you must tackle a problem from its beginning; you can think about or view the problem at any stage to get insight on it. Start in the middle!

10. No one is one hundred percent right all the time; give yourself permission not to have instant success. Clearly distinguish between real obstacles and the imagined ones that actually don't have to be overcome.

11. Once you have intuition about something, take action on your insights. Start investigating with the approach of "will this hunch logically work?" How can I check this out? Whom do I trust to review this solution with me?

12. Create some quiet "think time" in your schedule every day. Learn to meditate. With this quiet time, start to think metaphorically, in pictures, hunches, or feelings, using your imagination as much as possible. Be sure to write your thoughts down. Intuitive feelings tend to stay for a moment and then may be forgotten.

I would also like to add that your true connection with God may show up and give you answers while you are in the shower, cutting the grass, driving, or playing with your kids. Whenever your mind is open and receptive, it will get information—flashes of thought that just may answer your questions.

You might want to pay attention to when your mind is relaxed enough to hear your own inner wisdom, and then plan your problem-solving activities around that time schedule. I personally have some connection with the tile and water in my bathroom. Whenever I truly feel I must have an answer, I make sure to go take a long bath or a hot shower and, like magic, I receive answers! A friend of mine says that he gets his best information when he plays golf. So now he makes it a point to get on the golf course as much as possible when troubled with a problem.

Build Your Trust by Reviewing Your Past Successes

To motivate yourself to start to listen and act on your intuition, review all the times when you've acted on your instincts and were amazed at your success. You were listening to your intuition! Following your intuition requires you to love and have trust in yourself. Listening to those inner whispers and acting on them truly make a difference in how fulfilling your life can be.

Personally, I know in my heart that the most profound answers to my problems in life have always come from my intuition. My inner guidance has always led me to the right resources, or the right people who could give me the answers. Give yourself permission to let go of any fears and follow your natural connection to your God Source. Your faith in and trust of your God Source will deepen significantly as you cultivate the connection to that inner part of yourself.

Design affirmations and prayers that make you feel good and feel connected to your God Source. Here is an example of a prayer I use.

Prayer for Intuition

Dear God, assist me to hear your Divine Guidance. Direct me to use my life energy in the most productive, profitable, and God-directed ways possible. Give me confidence and faith that I am connected to you and all life. I know that I am always under God's direct inspiration. I make right decisions easily and effortlessly. So be it.

Power Tool Number 9— The Power of Prayer

Many people are confused about why praying is important for business. It's so easy to become consumed by materialism and forget our higher purpose in life. Contemporary life has led many of us to become self-centered and to ignore the teachings of great spiritual teachers such as Jesus Christ. The words of Jesus are just as powerful today as when he spoke them. Many people have forgotten the wisdom in the Bible such as:

Love your enemies, bless them that curse you, do good to them that hate you, and pray for those who despitefully use you, and persecute you.
Judge not, lest you be judged.
He that is without sin among you, let him cast the first stone.
As you sow, so shall you reap.
The kingdom of Heaven is within.
Ask and you shall receive, seek and you will find, knock and it shall be opened unto you.

When we follow Jesus' advice, our lives become more connected to God and we become better people. Prayer can bring you back to truth in your life. Cultivating a life of prayer will also bring you peace, serenity, enlightenment, contentment, and fulfillment.

There is not just one way to talk to God. There are many paths up the mountain, as they say, and everyone needs to find their own way on their own terms. We all must discover our higher purpose in life and our own mission. Any way you decide to pray is perfect for you but the most important thing is to take the time daily to talk to God and hand over your problems to a higher source so you can get guidance.

From India comes ancient spiritual literature such as the Bhagavad Gita, or "The Divine Song of the Divine Krishna." It says the key is to live a spiritual life and to have an awareness of our spiritual being, and to let that guide us at all times. We are to know that God is all-knowing, all-powerful, and omnipresent, within every atom of the universe, including ourselves. When we pray, we set in motion the ever-mysterious forces that create the answers to our prayers.

The Bible tells us: "Before they call I will answer." When you pray, you become in vibrational harmony with the answer you are seeking; you attract it to yourself. So the act of praying—that is, thanking God in advance for solutions and intuitive insight—attracts the results you want in your life by matching vibration levels with that good solution.

Prayer connects you with your God-consciousness. When you pray, you are enacting spiritual law. Your God Source is an indwelling presence within you and your prayers connect your consciousness with that presence. When you pray, you commune with your God Source; you sense it and feel it. The approach to your God Source is direct—through your own consciousness.

Speaking about prayer in his famous book *The Science of Mind*, Ernest Holmes says, "We can be certain that there is Intelligence in the Universe to which we may come, which will guide and inspire us, a love which overshadows. God is real to the one who believes in the Supreme Spirit, real to the soul that senses its unity with the Whole. Every day and every hour we are meeting the eternal realities of life and in such degree as we co-operate with these eternal realities in love, in peace, in wisdom, and in joy—believing and receiving—we are automatically blessed. Our prayer is answered before it is uttered."

Prayer is often said to be a mental approach to reality. We pray to demonstrate an invisible law which has power over the visible. It is often said that spiritual training begins with learning to pray. Develop the discipline of prayer because praying connects you to God and allows you to get answers, direction, and understanding.

Every day it would benefit you to take the time to pray for yourself and others. It has been suggested by great spiritual masters to always pray as you awake from sleep and pray as you go to sleep. These prayers connect you to your God Source and help open the door to your own wisdom.

Once you have prayed for someone or for an answer to a problem, step back and allow the world to answer you. Your answers may come when you have quieted yourself down and you are observing the messages around you. They may come in a book, a song, a conversation with someone else, a movie, or a television show. As they say, God works in mysterious ways, so be open for messages.

You can pray for wisdom or healing for yourself, or you can pray to send healing to the world. As a salesperson I have always prayed for all the people in my life, both personally and in my business. It keeps me connected to my purpose on Earth.

In the Twelve-Step Program, begun by Alcoholics Anonymous, the third step says, "I made a decision to turn my will and my life over to the care of God, as I understand God." The eleventh step says, "I sought through prayer and meditation to improve my conscious contact with God as I understand God, praying only for knowledge of God's will and the power to carry it out."

In his book *Visionary Business*, Marc Allen writes:

> Whenever you have a problem—business or personal—turn it over to the forces of creation, to God as you understand God. Most people call this process prayer, but you can call it anything you like. Just say, "Well, God, I put the problem in your hands—I'm turning it over to you. Just show me what your will is. Let me do your will." Turn everything over to God: let God work out the details. Just keep asking to do God's will, and your problems will dissolve. You will be shown, step by step,

intuitively, what to do. You never need to worry about your business once you really turn it over to God. For you aren't in charge of your business anymore—God is the new president and the chairman of the board as well. Just keep asking what God's will is, and you'll be guided in your business to do exactly the right thing for you. You might take the business in completely unexpected directions! It doesn't matter—God is showing you where and how to go. God is directing the show.

One of my personal favorite prayer books is *Your Needs Met*, by Jack and Cornelia Addington, who have created more than 150 prayers for all situations. This is from the first page of their book:

> There is no power in conditions;
> There is no power in situations.
> There is only power in God, Almighty.
> Pray for wisdom for yourself, pray to send healing to the world. God, within me right now. There is no person, place, thing, condition, or circumstance that can interfere with the perfect right action of God Almighty within me right now. I am pure spirit, living in a spiritual world. All things are possible to God through me.

I wanted to also share a business prayer from this same book, which you might want to refer to every morning before you start your business day:

> *I Bless My Work*
> Good morning, God! This business is your business. Everything You do is done easily, smoothly, and happily. Everyone who needs to know us is being drawn to us easily so that you may bless them through us. We give service, God's service, Love expressed through this office.
> Love permeates this office and is felt by everyone who crosses our doorstep. Love is our theme.
> Love blesses us and all who contact us.

Through Love, all those whom we need and those who need us are drawn to us as blessings unlimited!

Plenty of happy clients, successful transactions that bless and please everyone. Good Morning, God! We're ready to let you work through us today!

And so it is.

Everyone Needs Quiet Time

"All man's miseries derive from not being able to sit quietly in a room alone," the famous mathematician and philosopher Blaise Pascal observed. Most people cannot go into a room without turning on a television, radio, or computer. It's as though they are afraid to be alone in a room and think!

The average person does not want to actually "think" anymore, but allows the outside world to program his or her personal computer—the mind—on what to think and how to feel. In our noisy world we are constantly bombarded by loud music, sirens, trucks, jet planes, and lawn and construction equipment, which is seriously depleting our ability to hear ourselves think. With all the "other people's emotions" we subject ourselves to, it's no wonder that we are out of touch with our own feelings.

There is a silence in the space between your thoughts, where your true spiritual answers lie. This is the space where you can find—or plant—true personal peace. It is said that the average person has up to fifty thousand thoughts per day. Well, that doesn't leave much time for the silent spaces that bring us peace of mind, does it?

Spiritual teachers have taught us to go into the silence for all wisdom. When you can visit the silent spaces of your mind, you can open up an entire world of possibilities for your future. When you take the time to experience the silence, you are plugging into your God Source, acknowledging your connection with It. "Be still and know that I am God," it says in Psalm 46 of the Old Testament. All creation comes from the silence, and silence is what will recharge your life by removing stress, anxiety, and tension.

The purpose of this chapter is to urge you to demand more silence in your life so that you connect with your God Source. One of the most productive ways to create silence is to schedule time for it and make it a success habit. If you do not take this time to pray, you will be a "reactor" to life and find your day filled with the daily frustrations that come with the business world.

Create a Holy Day

I believe we are programmed, as salespeople, to believe we have to be available 24/7, and that is just not true. In fact, you teach your clients how to treat you and what to expect from you. If you allow them to have access to you at all times, you are training them to expect that access at all times. Should there be a time when they want you and you are not available, they will be disappointed in you.

If you try to be all things to all people, you are going to run yourself into the ground. To live a successful life you must have boundaries that support your views and values of life. You must listen to your heart about what is right for you, not what the world wants but what your individual soul wants. If you give your personal power away to the outside world, someone will be happy to suck the marrow right out of your bones. We have to take our power back. To be on the top of your game, you must take time to reflect, to plan, and to recharge in your daily life.

In our fast-paced world, many of us have forgotten the tradition of keeping the Sabbath, where you set aside one day per week as holy. On this Sabbath day you do no work and keep the day as a day of rest, rehabilitation, and prayer. Even the Bible says God needed a day to rest when the world was created. Yes, in one sense every day can be seen as holy, but if you take just one day a week and make it *your* holy day, you will see miracles in your output for the other six days of the week.

There is great value for your mind, body, and creativity to regularly set aside one day a week for rejuvenation, healing, and quiet time, to listen to your own wisdom-self. Answer this question honestly: When is the last time you truly took an entire Sabbath and did not do any work or chores? Don't you think you truly deserve one day of rest from the pressures of modern life?

Our culture, with its need to consume, now has everything available to us seven days a week, 24 hours a day. People who used to rest on Saturday or Sunday now spend those days shopping, working around the house, or paying bills. Our lives have become a course of endless work. This kind of nonstop "doing" eventually wears you down. As a society, we need to become conscious of the scope of damage that this stressful materialist cycle has had on our peace of mind, happiness, health, our communities, and our spiritual connection. Is this living in integrity with our values?

Are you a human being or a human doing? I'd like to suggest that you try an experiment for a month that, I hope, will become a habit. Choose just one day of the week on which you will not answer your phone; you have an answering machine for that. Do not make plans to work. Don't do any chores. Simply take this time to create a quiet reflective retreat wherein your God Source is your focus. On this day, only your family and loved ones are important. Do something that fills your soul up with the spiritual energy it needs to stay in touch with your God-self all week. There are no other rules. You get to make up the day to suit yourself. Just make the experiences of this one day a week *feel good*. You cannot get it wrong. Your God Source is always connected to you, no matter what. It's your intention that counts.

I also suggest that, from time to time, you create a retreat for a day or week to just do whatever gives your soul some good old "R and R"— relaxation and recreation. If you want to avoid unresourceful states of mind, you must take time to be still and listen to your inner self. Creating retreats allows you time to heal from the insanely busy world we live in; get back to nature and to who you really are without all the material aspects of the world. When you take time to listen to your God Source, you will find that most of your problems will resolve more easily and you will move away from operating in a crisis state of mind.

One of my coaching clients, Kelly, said that when he went back to the old-fashioned tradition of taking Sundays off, he saw an immediate improvement in his clarity, enthusiasm for life, and ability to be of service to his clients. Plus, he found that he had more compassion and patience and thus became a better father and husband. Kelly was a real estate agent and it was unheard of in his company not to work on Sundays. His boss told him he would never make a living not working on weekends. Kelly told his clients that he wanted to give them the best service possible but that Sunday was for his family and for God. He said that people respected him for his beliefs, and his business actually increased during the week, making it unnecessary for him to work on Sunday. He realized that time with his children was precious to him and that they were growing up so fast that if he did not schedule time with them now, he would never get it.

Further, by taking off just one day and devoting it to his family and spiritual work, he was motivated to start his own company. Today Kelly's business is one of the few real estate companies to advertise that Sunday is for families. He reported back to me that his agents are grateful to him for allowing them to have the day with their families and that they are one of the top companies in their city, with the reputation of high integrity and high-end sales records. Kelly also noted that since his agents knew that they were not going to show houses on Sunday they were motivated to organize appointments for other days of the week; thus they became more productive in a shorter time frame.

Before he passed away, my father told me that his biggest regret in life was that he did not spend enough time with his children. So the bottom line is, if you are not scheduling at least one day a week for rest and spiritual work, the world will not give it to you. You must draw a line in the sand and declare independence from the constant, draining cycles of work. Take the time to connect to your inner source.

It is a wise thing to learn from others' regrets, and I have learned from my own father's regret. I now take one day a week just for myself, my family, and my spiritual work. I don't look at e-mails, answer the phone, or do mundane chores. I spend time with my loved ones, walk in nature, meditate, pray, or write in my journal, and I maintain a state of great appreciation for my blessings. I take this quiet time to envision my future and write goals that I want to manifest in my life. Taking this one holy day brings me back to a centered feeling that assists me with the demands of the modern world. I go back to work feeling rested and with a sense of calmness that supports me all week long.

Meditation or Quiet Time

There is an old saying: Praying is talking to God; meditation is listening to God.

Over my years as an executive coach, I have suggested to all my clients that they meditate each day to shield themselves from the stress of the demanding world in which we live. Often, salespeople say, "When do I have time to meditate? What's the point?"

Meditation teachers say that one hour of meditation can be equivalent to a night's sleep. You will feel refreshed when finished. The real point is that by taking some quiet time or meditation time, you will achieve a quiet, relaxed state of mind. It is only when you are relaxed that you listen to your intuition (listening to God). When you are uptight, anxious or fearful thoughts may hold you back from listening to those inner urges of what you really want for yourself. Taking time to meditate aligns you with your highest and best good. Creating a time each day for inner reflection and listening to your God Source helps to reduce your stress, allowing you to feel more centered and in control of your life.

One of the greatest benefits of meditation is that it can remove you from your customary state of awareness and allow a new perception to flow into your consciousness. When practiced on a regular basis, meditation can relax and heal your body, making you more efficient mentally, creatively, and intuitively. Meditation also results in a more balanced, integrated, and harmonious personality. By maintaining a quiet time, we are stilling the ordinary, habitual chatter of our minds and relaxing the tensions in our stress-reactive bodies. It's a very simple process, yet at first your thoughts will take off in many directions, telling you that this is a waste of time and you should be doing something productive. At first you will experience tons of unrelated thoughts as you try to quiet your mind. Just stay centered and imagine yourself as an observer of all of this inner chatter and these unrelated thoughts. Within a short time you will be able to sit quietly and allow the silence, to allow the peace within yourself to come forward.

When you are at peace, your body's energy vibrates at a different speed from when you are stressed out or depressed. Since like energies attract, it certainly makes sense to align our bodies and minds with the peaceful clarity that will attract that same energy to us.

In his book *The Light of Consciousness*, Richard D. Mann describes meditation like this: "The body seems to be moved, purified; the imagery has an unfamiliar and awesome clarity; the spontaneous registry of what one's life and current experiences all imply at their core may take the form of searing insights. Even the stillness comes as a blessing and a discovery. Whatever happens, it continues to suggest a shift in the inner structure of one's consciousness."

I personally think being silent and peaceful is like having an invisible shield around you that negative energy cannot penetrate. A regular meditation practice can help to protect you from other people's crises and drama-laden behavior. You will find that as your meditation practice calms you, it has a soothing effect on those around you, too. You may feel less annoyed or negatively affected by common situations. The reason for the good feelings is that when you feel connected to your God Source, you feel at peace.

The point is to realize that your true power is internal and not external. If you make meditation an integral part of your daily life, it will become one of the more significant tools for controlling your life. When you meditate, you are quietly going within to discover the invisible intelligence and loving guidance that is always open and available to you. You are allowing yourself to be in direct contact with your God Source.

Dr. Wayne Dyer says it well in his book *10 Secrets for Success and Inner Peace:*

> I include the embracing of silence as one of my top ten secrets for inner peace and success, primarily because it's the only vehicle I know of for making conscious contact with God. God is that which is indivisible. There's only one omnipresent presence called God. This presence is everywhere and is a force that creates and sustains life. It can never be divided or cut up into pieces. There's only one power in the universe, not two. Everything in your experience as a human being appears to be in duality, however. Up exists because of its opposite, down.

Night exists because of day, right exists because of wrong. You've never seen a person with a front who doesn't have a back, an outside without an inside, a north pole of magnet without a south pole. Our physical world is a world of dichotomies and combinations of opposites, always divisible.

Silence, however, is the one experience you can have that's indivisible. You cut silence in half, and all you get is more silence. There's only one silence. Therefore, silence is your one way to experience the oneness and the indivisibility of God. This is why you want to meditate. This is how you know God rather than having to settle for knowing about God. You will find your answers in the silence.

When you go into a meditative state you can image or play out a problem or a difficult situation in your mind. You can ask for divine guidance about this situation. For example, suppose you have to deal with a difficult client but every time you are in this person's presence you get tongue-tied and frustrated. You could go into a meditative state and seek divine guidance by asking, "How can I act loving and serve this client to ensure a win-win outcome for everyone?" You will get answers, I promise.

When I meditate, I often ask about a problem for which I am trying to find solutions. I'll ask, "What is the lesson here? How can I benefit from this experience? How can I be of service? Whom do I need to forgive?" I view meditation as a valuable way to find solutions to real-life problems.

Getting Started

First let me share with you that there is no right or wrong way, no specific strategies that you must follow to start meditating. Learning to meditate is like learning anything else you do in life. You must want to do it and tell yourself that, by having quiet time in your life, you will access a valuable spiritual part of yourself that may have been hidden away.

The simple act of allowing your body and mind to relax is a form of meditating. For some people walking in nature, playing with pets, gardening, playing golf, or enjoying a hobby can lead to a state of mind that rejuvenates and allows the mind to stop the busy talk. I am going to offer some simple tips that will assist you to experiment with what works best for you.

In my experience, nature is one of the greatest places to find healing therapy. When you are feeling troubled, go out into nature and find peace and serenity. Nature has a marvelous ability to heal a troubled heart and mind. Make it a life habit to make time spent in natural surroundings a regular part of your routine. This can be anything from working outside in your yard to taking a walk. Allow your mind to relax and become silent; gently allow your spirit to commune with God.

I suggest that you show a form of honor to your God Source, that you consider creating a spiritually nourishing environment in your home and office, if possible. Adding music, flowers, or beautiful scents will assist the sensory side of your meditation process. Try to make your meditation location as peaceful as possible, with symbols and colors that create heart-opening feelings when you view them.

Some Simple Meditation Tips

1. Create a quiet environment, where you will not be disturbed for at least 20 minutes. You may want to play very soft instrumental music.

2. Wear loose, comfortable clothes or loosen your clothes so you are not distracted by them as you sit or lie in meditation.

3. Quiet the body. You can sit cross-legged, or sit in a chair with both feet flat on the floor, or you can lie on a mat/bed or the floor. Your spine should be erect/straight, but comfortable. Your body should be relaxed and at ease so you don't focus on it. You may want to start to quiet the body by doing some relaxation exercises. Try some deep-breathing exercises; begin with a deep inhalation, hold your breath for

a few seconds, then complete the cycle with a long slow exhalation. Your objective is to relax your mind and body.

4. Focus on a constant mental stimulus, such as a phrase, sound, or word repeated silently. You may close your eyes or fix your gaze on an outer focal point, such as a tree, a stream, a candle or anything that is pleasing to you. This simply helps you to shift away from your logical, externally oriented world.

5. Invoke a passive attitude. Don't work hard at meditating; you don't have to achieve anything—you're not in a competition. If distracting thoughts intrude, acknowledge them but let them pass through your mind; your goal is to be receptive. If you are uncomfortable, move; if you have an itch, scratch it, and return to the process. Again, you cannot do this incorrectly.

6. Allow yourself to just be in the quiet of your mind. Feel yourself going into your inner reality. Feel the centering, aligning, and balancing of the real you.

7. After your meditation period, bring yourself slowly and gently back into physical reality. Give yourself a few minutes to write down any thoughts or insights that came to you.

One of my clients, a stressed-out car dealership owner, told me that after about three weeks of meditation practice, he realized that he was now enjoying the wonderful connection he had been seeking. He reported to me that this one daily quiet time tool had benefited him more than all the professional therapy he had received over the years. He went on to say that he no longer operated in a crisis state of mind as he had in the past. He now takes 30 minutes every morning before he starts his day at the car dealership and he programs his mind to be in a peaceful state. His relationships at work and at home have changed for the better. His direct quote was, "I am not a dictator at work anymore and people seem so much more cooperative to me."

So, have you decided that you are willing to invest a few minutes a day to have quiet time to reinvent your life, to connect with your source of inspiration, comfort, and peace? Once you learn to meditate, it is important to train yourself to be able to do it at almost any time in order to center yourself, such as the five minutes right before an important sales call. Any time you feel under siege from the world, take a few minutes to go back to your core, to your God Source, so that you can make better choices and decisions.

Prayer for Quiet Time

Dear God Source,

I know I am always under your direct inspiration. There are no mysteries in God's kingdom and whatever I should know will now be revealed to me under grace. I am a perfect instrument to bring my perfect good into the world in perfect ways. Knowing this is true, I listen in the silence and know exactly what to do in all circumstances.

So be it.

Power Tool Number 10—
The Power of Setting Goals

Salespeople often manage their careers (and their lives) by crisis management. They get caught up in the difficulties of the daily grind and find it hard to pause to see the big picture. They forget to consider how they are using their life energies mentally, emotionally, physically, and spiritually.

When operating from crisis management mode, your life energy is consumed by reacting to other peoples' needs. The constant stress of crisis management mode is exhausting and drains you of your vitality and enthusiasm for life. Medical professionals agree that high doses of stress over a period of time can cause medical problems, both mental and physical. For those exhausted crisis managers, the simple act of writing personal goals is just more work and they find no time to do it.

Love, Nurture, and Protect Your Energy

You must be the captain of your own ship! If you truly want to co-create your life with your God Source, you cannot allow yourself to be controlled by the outside world and its needs and wants. You have to take care of yourself before you can take care of others, which takes some courage to do, but you cannot give what you do not have. If you are not willing to love, nurture, and protect yourself from the crisis demands of others, you will get sucked into the mud with them.

If you allow yourself to get into the crisis mindset, you cannot help another person in that same state of mind. To find creative, valuable avenues of action, you must be grounded, clear, and looking for solutions. You won't be able to see appropriate solutions while you are upset, freaked out, or frustrated, so just don't go there!

As a conscious salesperson, you can choose how to manage your career and life using spiritually conscious goals management. In this chapter I am challenging you to awaken the pioneer within yourself. You can learn to live without struggle and worry. Living your life by happenstance often leads to fruitless situations in which you feel powerless. Practicing the art of deliberate creation will bring you a conscious awareness of personal control and help you to optimize your choices.

The secret to manifesting what you want is to have one foot planted firmly in heaven and one foot planted firmly on earth. In other words, you use your inner thoughts, goal-setting activities, images, and self-talk to create your vision of your desired outcome; then, you take informed, well-timed action in the physical world. You must be the writer, set designer, head of casting, director, and actor in your own script of reality.

Yes, Setting Goals Is Important

Goal setting will transform you from a thinker with good intentions to an active achiever. You'll be more motivated, optimistic, and you'll feel more in control of your life than ever before. When you set clear goals you are giving your God Source a clear picture of what you want. Goals help us measure our lives and provide feedback to let us know how we are doing. They give us something specific to aim for with our life energy. For our goals to be fruitful, they must be anchored in something that arouses our courage, creativity, persistence, and sense of purpose.

Reassess Your Life . . . Really!

As a career coach I have found that some clients believe that God has ordained everything about their lives and that they cannot escape the mechanism of fate. The problem with that line of thinking is that if you believe life is predestined, you have placed a cap, an upper limit, on what is possible for your future. Any time you put limitations on what you can do you are sabotaging your possibility to transcend your old behaviors and create a new life for yourself. Nothing in life is predestined because you create your reality with your thoughts, actions, and emotions every single day as you co-create with your God Source.

One of the reasons for setting and reviewing goals is to reassess your progress on this journey of life. Whether or not you have achieved a high level of success in life, it is common to find that attainment of material possessions alone does not lead to a mature and healthy lifestyle. Create a mission and vision for yourself that drives you forward into your future. Don't be afraid to reassess and readjust your goals. Sometimes we make career choices that ultimately lose meaning for us because they were based solely on financial gain. With maturity, our lives tend to focus more on the need to be of service to others. Our sales work can encompass ethics, nobility, compassion, concern for the planet, and shared responsibilities for human problems.

The question of whether to choose a career based on materialistic or idealistic income is a question every spiritually conscious person must ponder. My view is that you can find a balance between altruistic purpose and material achievement. You can have the best of both worlds if you set your goals and intentions in that direction.

Goal-setting brings results because it is governed by specific mental laws. That to which you give your attention and in which you believe fully will become your reality. Because it is so important to your success as a conscious salesperson, I want to share with you some truly down-to-earth tools, as well as spiritual tools, for setting and achieving your goals.

Becoming a Deliberate Co-Creator

Spiritual masters teach that there are four basic steps to creating your life from a deliberate, conscious point of power. To become a deliberate creator of your life you must start to *feel* your life instead of just thinking about your life. Here's what to do:

Step One: Identify what you do *not* want—period. Get clear about what does not work for you in life or in your work. Write it down.

Step Two: Knowing what you definitely don't want, identify what you know that you do want. Write it down.

Step Three: Close your eyes and find the good feelings that you associate with your desired goals. Enjoy this state of feeling; enjoy feeling like you have exactly what you want. Write down how you feel so that you can remember it easily.

Step Four: Write out your goal(s); create a clear intention to bring these goals to yourself. In your mind's eye, create a vision of the end result, of the way you just felt in Step Three. Let go and let your God Source make it happen. Create a daily mental rehearsal of your upcoming success.

These steps put an end to the long-held notions that struggle and blame are the causative factors in our lives. If you will simply change the way you think, you will change the way you feel. Changing the way you feel changes the frequency of your body/mind vibrations and that changes the way you attract life events.

Remember to see yourself as a magnet and be sensitive to the way you feel about what you see, hear, and do every day. Developing the skill to be aware of where your emotional energy is can help you make better decisions. If you are feeling good about a particular path or decision, that means you are in tune with your God Source and have access to spiritual guidance and wisdom. If you are feeling bad about a particular path or decision, you are out of sync with your spiritual connection and will not have that wise guidance available to you on that path. You cannot be thinking fearful and frustrating thoughts and expect to have positive powerful assistance.

Like Attracts Like

Thoughts that are similar are magnetically attracted to each other. The universe doesn't actually "hear" words, it senses your vibrations. Your negative thoughts actually are attracting more of whatever made you upset! That is why, as a conscious salesperson, you must focus on what makes you feel good; once you are in that good-feeling place, you can start deliberately attracting what you want into your life.

Think Big

Your success or lack of it reflects what is in your mind. Your sales success is the sum of all the thoughts you have had about it. If your life seems small, it's probably because your dominant visual picture of your life has been small. If you think big you will get big results. Small thinking is sure to get small results. Conscious salespeople map out a new way of thinking bigger that attracts to them new resources and options.

At a very young age my mother told me that if I did not know what to do in a social environment, I should to look around for the most successful person in the room and copy her or him. This advice has served me very well both personally and in business. When I first got into sales I did what most salespeople do: call on an account, sell them, and then service the account well, hoping for repeat business. I was always trying to find new accounts and going through the entire process again and again. I started to notice that the most successful salespeople seemed to work on big accounts, not a hundred small ones. Now, I am not a person who believes you should put all your eggs in one basket, but I did see that working on big accounts that had multiple locations was a more effective and efficient way of doing business.

After I stopped selling radio advertising, I started working for and eventually owned part of a company called Background Music Service of Tidewater. We sold electronic sound systems, commercial phone systems, and paging systems for commercial buildings. In the past the salespeople had always called on the mom-and-pop businesses, such as dentists, small retail shops, and business offices. When I came on board, I decided to dream really big and go for supermarket and drugstore chains, entire shopping centers, and office buildings. I will admit to you that it takes longer to make a sale, involves lots more red tape, and there are more gatekeepers to pass and more hoops to jump through for the bigger sale. However, once I did all that work to sell one location, if they liked my work, I would then be in line for multiple sales. Thus, I would have created relationships with large companies that would bring in much more revenue than the small accounts.

Every day, I visualized myself working with really big names in the chain store business. I imaged myself flying to the corporate headquarters of some of those big businesses and saw them sign the contracts for several locations at once. I began to see my commission checks in my mind, and they were huge!

Some of these accounts took as long as several years to sell, but I stayed with the visions of working with the big boys until I made it happen. Once I was in with these big accounts I made triple the money I had earned before, and now I was actually doing less service work. Thinking big leads to taking more risks, asking for what you want, and laying a foundation of future success. The old saying "you cannot win if you don't play" is so true. As a salesperson you must leverage your time, experience, and knowledge in the best way possible. Don't let anyone tell you it can't be done. Of course, you must tailor your sales approach to your market, but why not think big? Why not think outside the box of your old sales model?

Let me share some action steps that can show you fast results and give you the confidence to really go for what your heart is asking for in your life.

Get Excited about Goal Setting

Since the first step to reaching a dream is having one, start asking yourself, what do you want in life? These desires must be realistic and obtainable. Listen to your intuition when setting goals for your sales career. To motivate yourself to get into goal setting, you must not try to reinvent the wheel; adapt the successful techniques of others to fit your own style, personality, and profession.

Goals must be well thought out to be sure you will attract what you actually want. The old saying "be careful what you wish for" is true for your goals, also. Don't ask for a pony if you live in the city where you cannot keep it. Also, make sure your goals are congruent with your inner callings. Don't set a goal to be the sales manager of your company if you don't want the pressure of the job.

When you are emotionally excited, you can move mountains by focusing your life energy in the direction of what you want. The more you are excited, jazzed up, and turned on by your goals, the more you vibrate to a higher level and the faster you attract to yourself what you are excited about.

Crystallize Your Thinking

Your goals need to be specific, measurable, and realistic. Exactly how much money do you want to earn? How many new accounts do you want to add? How can you create more word-of-mouth advertising? What can you do to make yourself more attractive to clients?

Develop a Sincere Desire for the Things You Want

Desire is the starting point for all achievement. It's the greatest motivator of every human action. Again, dream big! The universe has a way of delivering to you exactly what you ask for, so ask for what you want. Put pictures of what you want around you where you will see them. Say out loud, with emotion and enthusiasm, daily, "I am now easily and effortlessly attracting everything I want and need."

Develop a Plan for Achieving Your Goal

The difference between a "wish" and a "goal" is that the goal is written down. Deliberate concentration is like a laser beam—it can cut through any obstacle in your path. You must create a plan and work your plan daily.

Distinguish between Goals and Activities

A goal is the specific end result that you want to manifest in your life. Keep in mind that activities are those things that you do to achieve your goals. Always be aware; don't get stuck in the activities and forget what the goal is!

Create a Deadline for Your Goal

Without deadlines your brain doesn't have a clear picture of what you want created. Deadlines have a magical way of motivating us to produce results. They allow us to break down our long-term goals into short-term ones that feel attainable. Write your goals and deadlines down in a notebook so you can review them weekly and chart where you are and what you need to do to reach your goals. Affirm "this goal is in divine perfect timing for all concerned."

Picture the End Result

I love to say in my seminars that famous wise saying—success is not like a book where you start at the beginning, read the middle, and finish with the end. Success is achieved backward; you must look at what you want in detail and then listen to your intuition on what paths to take and what tools to use.

Leonardo da Vinci emphasized the importance of setting clear goals and following through to completion to be successful in anything. He wrote repeatedly, "Think well to the end" and "Consider first the end." Whatever is dominant in our thoughts is going to come to pass. Our modern-day muse, Stephen Covey, in his famous book *The Seven Habits of Highly Effective People*, says, "Begin with the end in mind."

When you focus on positive results you are putting your vibration in the same wave as the physical positive results you desire. When we focus on the crisis of the moment, we are simply creating more crises for the future. When setting goals you must focus on the solutions and outcomes that you want, not on the problems.

Make Your Goals Yours

Don't set a goal for yourself that your spouse (or anyone else for that matter) wants for you. You will never be successful achieving goals that are not motivated by your own desires. Don't compare your goals with other salespeople's goals, either. Everyone is unique and you must go for your own goals.

Your Power Is Now

Write your goals as if they have already occurred. "I now earn $ _____," "I now weigh _____ pounds," rather than "I want to earn $ _____" or "I want to weigh _____." This allows your mind to see the specific end result.

Develop Confidence in Yourself and Your Abilities

Stay "sold on yourself." Listen to motivational CDs or audiotapes daily in your car. Control your self-talk. Focus on your strengths instead of your weaknesses. Recognize and honor your powers instead of your problems.

Develop a determination to follow through on your goals regardless of obstacles, circumstances, or criticism. Don't allow one bad sales call or bad day to discourage you from going for what you want.

Keep Your Goals to Yourself

If you are excited and charged up about your dreams, you'll want to share this information. Don't! Too often, you'll hear how everyone else has failed while trying to do what you want to do. Their negative energy and opinions may sabotage your enthusiasm and faith in your own abilities. It is wise to share your inner feelings and desires only with someone who is like-minded, believes in you, and wants you to be successful. Choose your confidants carefully.

Review Your Goals Monthly

The first of every month is the best time to review your goals for achievement and to set new goals as appropriate. The simple act of writing your goals brings them closer to you. I suggest that you write your goals once a week to refresh your vision of what you want. You could spend a few minutes mentally rehearsing the achievement of the goal, to get in touch with the feeling of achievement. Be honest with yourself about which goals are only paper dreams. These actions will attract the thoughts, inspiration, and assistance that you will need to achieve your desires and goals.

Be Persistent

Persistence is the real key to successful goal achievement. Don't allow yourself to become distracted with excuses about why things can't be done. Excuses are the enemies of goal achievement. Rather, focus on what you are going to do to create your own future. Everything you do now seeds your future. Your point of power is at this minute in time, so persist in your goal-oriented behavior in this minute, then the next, then the next!

Persistence is the key to long-term success in anything. It's been said that most people give up just as they were about to be successful. You must be willing to be bad at something before you can become good at it. No one is a pro at sales in the beginning. We all have to practice our presentations, expand our knowledge, sincerely want to be the best possible, and detach from rejection.

Assign a Timeline to Your Goals

The purpose of any goal is to determine precisely what it is you want. You must decide on a time frame for having this new goal. This time frame or deadline will create for you a sense of urgency or purpose, which will give you a sense of awareness of where you are and will prevent inertia or procrastination. These time frames will also act as a motivator to see results. Ultimately you do let God determine the perfect timelines.

Define Your Goals in Terms of Steps and Directions

Goals don't just achieve themselves! True goal achievement happens because you take one step at a time toward the goal. All progress comes from well-chosen, interval steps that are realistic and can produce measurable results. Most people set goals and don't take the time to discern what steps to take before setting out to achieve them. As you set your goals, take time to brainstorm with others the important steps to take and their correct order.

Choose Goals That You Are Willing to Work For

Goals must be concerned with aspects of your life that you can control and that you will take action to achieve. When you take the time to identify your goals, be sure you are willing to strive for what you want. You may dream of being a rock star but, in real life, are you willing to do what it takes to make it in that world? Focus your thoughts and actions on what you can create in your world.

Plan Strategies That Help You Stay on Course

Salespeople who are massively successful realistically assess their obstacles and resources. Create a strategy for navigating the obstacles. Many salespeople think that their willpower, alone, will help them reach their goals. If you take an honest look at your own history, you will find that willpower can be unreliable because it is based on your emotions.

Life offers salespeople many temptations to get off course from their goals. Be sure that your days include plenty of task-oriented behavior. Pay attention to your strategies in three areas: your environment, your schedule, and your accountability. The course of progress for each must be monitored so that all three will support you in achieving your goals.

Set Up Accountability for Your Progress

The most impressive salespeople I have ever met periodically make reports on their progress. Find someone in your life that you trust and who is willing to assist you to be accountable. This is someone who can say to you, "So, did that behavior serve your goals or hinder them?"

Many salespeople con themselves by doing busywork instead of profit work in their businesses. Keep in mind that there are real consequences for not doing the right work at the right time. The old saying that "God helps people who help themselves" is true. If you want to be successful, you need to do the right things that bring right results. If you don't know what the right things are, study people who have become successful in your field. Model their behavior.

Take Action

Sally Berger says, "The secret of getting ahead is getting started." The people who persistently take purposeful, directional action are the ones who achieve their goals. Every day you must take action on at least one of your goals. Reward yourself at the end of the day for moving ahead. Do not just sit and think about what you want to do.

Do it—take action!

Rekindle Your Passion

Salespeople who love what they do are excited to get to work in the morning. If you have lost your passion for your work, sit down and write a list of the positive things about your work and business. Post this list in a place where you can see it daily to remind yourself every day that *you* are choosing how to spend your life energy. Salespeople who live and breathe what they want seem to get there faster. It's a wise salesperson who is invested in both the journey and the goal. Don't lose sight of your partnership with your God Source and remember that your work is your ministry.

Be Flexible

They say the most successful salespeople are the ones who are flexible enough to understand that even the best-laid plans may need to be changed. When working on your goals make sure you are open-minded and flexible enough to start over or alter your direction. Be open to viable alternatives from others. One of our true powers in life is to be flexible so that the universe can work in mysterious ways to assist us!

Be Self-Controlled and Self-Managed

Successful salespeople realize that *they* are their own most important resource in achieving their dreams and goals. They know they must actively manage their mental, emotional, physical, spiritual, and financial energy to achieve their goals.

Be a Lifelong Learner, Curious and Open-Minded

Exposing yourself to more and more information about success in your field is the key to becoming a conscious salesperson. Create a plan for lifelong learning. There is only one way to get answers—by asking questions. Learn one new thing every day. Expose yourself to seminars, books, and recordings while commuting. Learning new things keeps you and your business healthy. And it's fun to feed your mind with useful information. Knowledge has a cumulative effect and adds to your resources.

Take Smart Risks

Successful salespeople take more risks than the average salesperson because they are willing to get out of their comfort zones. It may be scary to go into the unknown and leave behind the safe and familiar world but, to have more in life, you have to take smart risks. Before you take a risk, be sure to examine the downside as well as the upside, and decide if you can live with either. Be honest with yourself about living with the possible results of your decisions.

Know Your Priorities and Values

Successful salespeople always take the time to manage their challenges by knowing exactly what is most important. Commit to managing your time so you are always spending it on the tasks that are most likely to quickly achieve your goals.

Create a Support Team

Realize that you cannot be all things to all people. You must surround yourself with a group of people who want you to succeed. And these people should have abilities, skills, and talents that you do not have so they can assist you in creating a balanced business. Reward the people in your life who help you achieve your goals, so that they continue to help you get where you want to be. The truth in life is that no one becomes successful all alone.

Build a team of people that truly appreciates you and wants to assist you in achieving your goals and dreams. As a conscious salesperson, make sure you work in a partnership where you can turn conflict into harmony. Always treat others the way you want to be treated. Following the Golden Rule will make people want to work for and with you. Allow your God Source to be your greatest support. You are never alone. You are always loved.

Thank God in Advance

Thank your God Source daily for manifesting your goals. When you thank God for what you want before you get it, you are programming your mind and the universe to accept that you already have it. Then you start to vibrate at the same frequency as your goal, which makes the law of attraction work for you, bringing you exactly what you want.

At this point, if you have followed all these suggestions, it's time to simply trust your God Source to bring your highest and best into your life. Train yourself to stay out of the "how-to" business of manifesting your goal. Let that go; it's not your job. You have now turned over the details to your God Source and can allow your life to unfold in an adventure. You are allowing your God Source to guide you in the direction that is for your highest and best good. Allow yourself to feel deserving, for you are a perfect child of God.

Prayer for Goal-Driven Behavior

I am one with my God Source now.

My God Source is filling me now with the power to define, clarify, and carry through with exactly the right and perfect goals for my life.

I now pursue only those goals about which I have received clarity and direction from my God Source.

With God as my business partner I have all the energy, focus, and right ideas I need to succeed in my goals.

Thank you, God. Amen.

Power Tool Number 11—
The Power of a Full Toolbox

As a conscious salesperson, four things are required for success in sales: the proper attitude, sales knowledge, selling skills, and your connection to your God Source. I like to think of it as the success triangle with a support line under it called God. In this chapter I want to share with you more mindsets, or power tools, that will guarantee success in the sales world and your personal life. These tools will assist you in staying grounded for success. As I have said before, you have to have one foot in heaven and one foot on Earth to truly be balanced in your sales career.

The Power of Maintaining a Positive Attitude

Success in life is 80 percent attitude and 20 percent aptitude. It's our attitude that will advance our careers and enhance our futures. Robert Schuller said, "Success doesn't come the way you think it does, it comes from the way you think." This type of mindset allows us to respond positively rather than reacting negatively during stressful times. With a positive attitude, we empower ourselves to make things happen instead of sitting around waiting for something to happen. Adopt an "if there is no wind, row" kind of attitude.

Intending to have a positive attitude enables us to respond to our opportunities, to rise up in hope to meet overwhelming challenges, to courageously overcome great obstacles and setbacks. Controlling your attitude is the key to controlling your vibrational harmony and to successful attraction of the life you'd like to have. We have more leverage for any kind of success when we expect to win. Salespeople who are optimists know they have the abilities and resources to handle any challenge. Thomas Edison said, "If we did all the things in life we were capable of doing, we would literally astound ourselves." We are self-fulfilling prophecies; our focus always becomes our reality.

My first sales manager in the radio business had this quote on the wall in his office: "The truth is, real difficulties can be overcome. It is only the imaginary ones that are unconquerable." You get in life what you focus on. If you dwell on limitations, you will reach them. Optimistic salespeople know that difficult situations or adversity brings out hidden resources and capabilities. Choose to see opportunities where others choose to see problems. Make an internal decision to excel and rise to any occasion.

As a conscious salesperson, you must choose to be proactive in life, and not let life just happen to you. Be driven by your desires and goals and not by outside circumstances. You are not a victim of circumstances; you make your own environment because you are the creator of your life, using your thoughts and actions and spiritual assistance.

Having a positive and spiritual attitude gives you fantastic selling ability because clients respond positively to salespeople who understand their needs, desires, and interests. You will always stand out in the crowd because of your integrity and desire to be of service.

The Power of Controlling Your State of Mind

I was working on a multiunit sale and it had come down to my company's product or my competitor's. The prospect had told us both we were neck-and-neck for prices, time lines, and service. He was convinced our services were equal in terms of value, price, and resources. The prospect couldn't decide, so he invited me and my competitor in for a final last meeting with all of the decision-making committee. Just before we went into the meeting my competitor's cell phone rang and he took the call. It was impossible not to overhear that he was getting very upset and frustrated; clearly he was having an argument with the caller.

I noticed his negative energy, took the opportunity to excuse myself, and went out into the hallway; I closed my eyes and imagined the sale going to me. I saw myself shaking the hand of everyone in the room and thanking them for using my firm as they signed the agreement. I got myself into a good feeling place and just imaged going back to my office and handing the paperwork to my sales manger; I even saw the look of excitement on his face. I saw my sales manager write my sale up on the sales board in our office. I stayed with the feeling of success for about twenty-five seconds, filling in all the details of me winning the contract. Then I just said a prayer. "Dear God, allow my company to serve this client and create a very rewarding working relationship for all parties involved. So be it."

Finally, when my competitor and I went into the boardroom for our meeting, I felt that I had the edge; I felt confidently relaxed and was able to answer all their questions easily and thoroughly. I noticed my competitor's presentations were forced, that he looked and acted stressed.

The upshot was, I got the contract and I was told later that the defining moment came when the committee took note that I was relaxed and confident while making my presentation. I am convinced that because my competitor took that negative phone call, it ruined his vibrational energy. He was in harmony with frustration where I was in harmony with victory.

I think this story makes very clear that you want to put yourself in a positive state of mind before you call on a client or deal with a prospect. It only takes a few seconds to pull yourself away from the others; you can do it in your car before you walk in, in the restroom, in a hallway. Just make a ritual of seeing with your mind's eye exactly what you want at the end of the meeting. Remind yourself that you are there to serve, and call on your God Source to assist you.

For me personally, when I married my God Source with my sales career, my life totally changed for the better. I lost that feeling of being desperate to make a sale. I started to trust my connection to something much bigger than I could ever imagine.

This powerful energy we call God has created everything in our world. With our free will, we get to co-create with God, focusing our thoughts and positive emotions in the direction that attracts to us our desired goals.

The Power of Forgiveness

One of the most important tools to creating a more successful sales career is to be aware of how you are using your life energy. If you're exhausting your energy holding on to past grudges, anger, guilt, or any negative feelings, you're wasting precious life energy and blocking yourself from sales.

Using your life energy to hold on to negative thoughts prevents you from creating new ideas and from having the energy to take action on them. Holding on to angry feelings, frustrated feelings, or get-even feelings puts you in vibrational harmony with negative energy. Clients will feel turned off by your negative energy. The remedy and antidote are to forgive yourself, and to forgive other people. But most of us have a hard time with the concept of forgiveness, don't we?

You do not have to condone the wrongs you perceive others to have done; just shift your perspective. Most people are not trying to hurt you with their actions, but are simply doing the best they know how. If they knew better, most of them would do better. Let go of your perceptions of wrongdoing and you will free your energy to move forward with your life.

Forgiveness has been taught by every spiritual leader since the beginning of written time. It is a component of every major religion. Keep in mind the exercise of forgiveness is really for you. You're not forgiving someone for their sake, but for yours. You are giving yourself a gift of positive vibrational energy by forgiving your trespassers. Forgiveness is releasing the thoughts, grudges, and anger that take up your time and eat up your energy. Through forgiveness and release of negative energy, your power to attract the good things you want in your life increases.

You probably have a story about how something great would have happened in your life *if* someone had not done something to interfere with your success. We end up blaming others for our lack of achievement. When you take a spiritual perspective you realize that you are either part of the solution or part of the problem. My life energy is intimately attached to the energy pattern of my dominant thoughts. I am 100 percent responsible for the results in my life. If I am vibrating at a low frequency, feeling upset and angry, I will repulse positive sales and receptive people because we will not be a vibrational match.

The Power of Self-Discipline

Successful salespeople take time to acquire and develop whatever skills are needed for psychological, professional, and spiritual growth. We must constantly challenge ourselves to utilize the great potential that is within us. It takes a tremendous amount of courage to go beyond our comfort zones, to expand our boundaries, and claim new territories of the mind and spirit for ourselves. As Robert Lewis Stevenson said, "To be what we are, and to become what we are capable of becoming is the only end of life."

Conscious salespeople are willing to undertake whatever educational processes will give them the knowledge to succeed in the future. The main theme in their lives is that choice, not chance, determines their destiny. They affirm that they have the power to be the master of their own fate.

You must use your personal self-discipline to develop positive mental thoughts and assume responsibility for your own future. In his famous book *As a Man Thinketh*, James Allen says, "Circumstance does not make the man, it reveals him to himself." The next time you deal with adversity, temporary defeat, or failure, remember that you may have no control over unpleasant circumstances, but you do have control over your reaction to those circumstances. You must search for the seed of opportunity, which is carried in every experience of adversity.

Self-discipline is sometimes called "willpower." Success requires the application of personal self-discipline, to do the right things with your time and life energy. When asked to explain his genius, Thomas Edison replied, "Genius is one percent inspiration, and ninety-nine percent perspiration." He also said that "A genius is a talented person who does his homework."

When you use your self-discipline, you leverage your thoughts, intentions, and actions to create your future. Your destiny truly is the consequence of your daily decisions. It is the decisions you make in your life, not the circumstances of your life, that will determine your outcome in the world.

Having self-discipline means having the courage to change your daily habits and question your focus. Self-discipline requires persistence and determination and an awareness of the use of your life energy. Using self-discipline will improve your chances to create new opportunities, to strengthen your self-esteem, and to utilize your potential.

Developing self-discipline helps you to utilize your inner power to make better decisions as you shape your life. You know that you have the power to create new options for yourself, to reinvent yourself simply by demanding more of yourself. Self-discipline, added to your repertoire of other spiritual and sales tools, gives you an advantage over your competition.

The Power of Focus

Focus is one of the keys to success, but many people have a hard time focusing their energy and thoughts in a clear direction. One day they are heading for a particular goal, and then six months later that goal is forgotten and they are heading off in another direction. Someone or something has distracted their attention from the original goal. They lost track or just did not follow their plan to achieve the goal and simply went off after something else.

You must create boundaries to help you focus your thoughts and attention toward your goals.. This is to guard your mind from negative sources that may defeat your positive thinking and to create for yourself a vibrational match that will attract to you what you want.

If you were to get only one insight from this book, which if you believed it with all your heart and acted upon it with all your might would make you wealthy beyond your wildest dreams, it would be this: *You have the power within yourself to create your own reality by simply focusing on exactly what you want with positive feelings of expectancy.*

I personally thank the power of focus for assisting me in creating a prosperous and blessed life. When I focus on an important project or goal I become almost obsessed. The strong focus I use on my goals makes the goal come into reality faster. Intense efforts will bring intense results. Small efforts bring small results.

Case in point: I had to make changes in my life and reduce my travel for speaking engagements to devote the time to the new goal of writing this spiritually focused sales book. For a while, I had to let go of my preference for my home to look like "house beautiful." All other major projects had to go on hold while I focused my creative energy into this book. And I hung up a big yellow cardboard sign in the entrance of my house. On it was written in large Magic Marker letters:

Attention: I am writing a new book—all bets are off!

This silly sign is a reminder to the people around me of "our deal." The deal I make with my family, friends, and staff is not to expect me to be my normal self while I am writing. Please allow me this time to work on this project without interrupting my flow of energy unless it is an absolute necessity.

In no way am I suggesting that you go as "off the charts" as I do when I write, but you do need to make some sacrifices to allow yourself the time and space to focus on your goals. Ask yourself during the day, "Where is my focus? Am I focusing on my priorities or doing busywork that is not productive or profitable?" Be honest with yourself about how you use your time and your mind.

The Power of Time Management

> Nothing is worth more than this day.
>
> —Goethe

Why do I write about time management in a book about spiritual power tools? It's important to respect and honor yourself and others by having a time management system in place. One of my greatest mentors is Dan Kennedy, who is hands down one of the most brilliant writers of our time when it comes to delivering valuable information to people who want to be outrageously successful. I highly suggest that you read Dan's *NO B.S. Time Management for Entrepreneurs.* This book can sharpen your awareness of how to use your time more effectively.

As a conscious salesperson, you must first take care of yourself, create boundaries, and set limits on how you spend your time *before* you take care of the rest of the world's needs. This is a very important spiritual tool to have—*clarity.* You cannot give to others what you do not have. If you allow yourself to be the rescuer of the world, you will find quickly that all your resources will be exhausted and you are not able to save the world alone.

All of your time is fed, fueled, or financed by at least one of your energy sources, whether mental, physical, emotional, or spiritual. The choices you make on how you spend time—how you use your life energy—will have consequences. Since your life is financed by the resources you have available to you, you must be conscious of how you spend the energy you have. If you overspend your life energy in ineffective ways, you will burn out, be too tired to be successful, and therefore be unable to contribute much to others.

Review who and what you allow to utilize your energy resources. If you find that you have energy drains, do something about it—now! Create a plan and goals for your personal and business time, or someone else will find a use for it. You must value your time and life energy as your most important resources.

Time is the most precious asset anyone can have in the sales world. You need quality time to make quality-conscious decisions. You need time to create, think, invent, and plan. You need time to develop sales, marketing, management, and profit breakthroughs. You need time to network and build relationships. Time is needed to gather and assimilate information and solve problems. And that's just the time needed for your business life! We haven't touched on the need for quality time for rest and rejuvenation, for hobbies and fun, for continued education.

Taking back control of your time can be the single biggest secret of extraordinary personal, spiritual, financial, and sales success. Controlling the use or abuse of your time by others is the single most important factor in utilizing your life energy effectively. Since you are the creator of your life, why not become very conscious of the passing of time and be aware of how you spend your time and who and what uses up your time? As Dan Kennedy says, "If you don't know what your time is worth, you can't expect the world to know it either." As a conscious salesperson, what value do you place on your time? Are you conscious and guarded about where your time is spent or do you allow others to steal your time in unproductive meetings, shooting the breeze, or just avoiding productive activities? Are you hanging on to clients and accounts that consume far more time and energy than they can ever be worth? It doesn't take a rocket scientist to figure out that when you waste time or allow others to waste your time, you have less time to focus your energies in areas that would bring you joy and prosperity.

How do you use your precious resource of time to manifest what you want? Most people are reactors to life, letting time run them. It's important to be conscious of how you are creating your life by choosing to be a co-creator of your own life. You do that by creating boundaries and a time management plan. You can only gain control of your life when you gain control over your time and how you utilize it.

The Power of Appreciation

By now you have realized that, as a conscious salesperson, you must stop talking and thinking about any type of economic lack and limitation because of the effects on your subconscious. The best way to avoid the poverty mindset is to start to appreciate the richness of the life that you already live right now.

Realize just how blessed you already are in this very moment. Start a list of the blessings you enjoy, even the simple ones you may have been taking for granted. Many people don't focus on what is good in their lives and careers until they've lost them. Become conscious of all of your blessings right now and see how thankful you can feel.

When you take the time to identify what is good in your life, you are using your mind and your energy to feel good, and to feel good about others in your life. That good-feeling state has a huge impact on your overall state of mind. If you feel happier and more content, you have more confidence. When you have more confidence, you'll naturally be more willing to step forward in your career and your life. You'll be more optimistic and creative; you'll see more new ideas and ways to capitalize on those ideas. This is the mindset that gives you the opportunity to make more money, meet better contacts, and create new relationships for better sales. And it all started with your feelings of gratitude for your current blessings!

It's amazing how most people overlook cultivation of the feeling of gratitude. It can truly beautify the way you perceive your own world. When you carry within you thoughts of gratitude and appreciation, they radiate outwardly into your world and will attract like results into your life. You have to *feel* successful, worthy, and blessed to be able to attract these things into your life.

The Power of Choice

Your power of choice is your one true personal power. It is your greatest ally as you design your destiny, for you are ultimately shaping your destiny with the choices you make every single day. In fact, your power of choice is the only power you have that can ensure you will create a life that fits your own unique personality and needs.

Choose to make important decisions in a state of connection to your inner power, your God Source. Connecting to your God Source will give you clarity and insight. When in doubt, don't do anything, if possible. Simply going into a quiet state of mind for a few moments will assist you to see the "truth" of any situation and make a wise decision.

The Power of Persistence

You know by now that persistence is an essential factor in transforming desire into reality. By developing the perseverance to go beyond what we comfortably know, we expand our boundaries to claim for ourselves new territories of the mind and spirit.

Having persistence allows you to keep moving forward, even when you don't see immediate positive results. It is the internal commitment to withstand setbacks and not give up. Persistence is a very spiritual tool because it involves faith in yourself and in your God Source.

Alexander Graham Bell said this about persistence: "What this power is I cannot say. All I know is that it exists and becomes available only when a man is in that state of mind in which he knows exactly what he wants and is fully determined not to quit until he finds it." John D. Rockefeller said, "I do not think there is any other quality so essential to success of any kind as the quality of persistence; it overcomes almost everything, even nature."

The Power of a Strong Work Ethic

As a farmer's daughter living on a working farm, I learned a great work ethic from my parents. Growing up on a farm gave me skills that have assisted me in ways I could have never developed from a so-called easier lifestyle. We were very self-sufficient; a million things can happen on a farm that has a large number of animals, unpredictable weather, and farm crops and we had to rely on our own wits to figure out what to do in case of a problem. I learned early to be a solution finder and to have the discipline to do the right things with my time because both people and animals were depending on my actions. Learning to utilize my life energy effectively has enabled me to use my talents, knowledge, and skills to earn a great living in the sales world.

As an executive coach, I find that the people who become truly great at the sales game have a great deal of self-discipline and a good work ethic to leverage for success. People with a great work ethic love what they do and feel passion for it, so it doesn't really feel like work.

The Power of Sales Skills and Knowledge

Conscious salespeople are lifelong learners—curious, open-minded, and open to change. Make a special effort to observe what strategies other salespeople are using. Look for ideas to improve yourself and your abilities. Observe, adapt, and then take action based on your new knowledge.

Start today to use your dead time productively. Read everything you can get your hands on that will empower you to be more educated in your field. Read whenever you are waiting for appointments. Instead of wasting your precious life energy watching mindless television, read materials that will advance you toward your goals.

Salespeople who are at the top always invest in themselves with coaches, books, audio and video learning tapes and CDs, and educational seminars. You must collect knowledge and skills that will assist you to be outstanding in your profession. Socrates said this about education:

> Whom, then, do I call educated? First, those who control circumstances instead of being mastered by them; those who meet all occasions manfully and act in accordance with intelligent thinking; those who are honorable in all dealings, who treat good-naturedly persons and things that are disagreeable; and furthermore, those who hold their pleasure under control and are not overcome by misfortune; and finally, those who are not spoiled by success.

Conscious salespeople understand exactly what selling is about:

- It is a response to the desires, needs, and interests of consumers through the creation of products and services to fulfill their wishes.
- It is responding to the consumers' need to know by inviting them to learn about these products and services. It is the consumers responding to an invitation to learn what a product and service can do for them.
- It is an invitation to the consumers to purchase what they wish to buy.
- It is the consumer responding positively, or answering with a promise to pay for a product or service.

The Power of Honoring Your Clients and Customers

The best way to get people to buy from you is for you to be responsive to their needs, interests, and desires. Today's consumers are intelligent, alert, highly selective, and independent in their thinking and the key to success is understanding, addressing, communicating, and delivering what the customer wants, not what you have to sell. Let me make you a promise: If you will apply this concept of putting the customer first and allow to it become a vigorous positive force in your sales approach, I promise you will see an instant and marked upturn in your sales production and referrals.

I know from my own experience that one of the greatest thrills in life is to shake hands with a client and walk away with a signed agreement and a check. Yet, as exciting as that moment can be, the conscious salesperson knows there is much more to be done. Reinforcing the sale, assuring satisfactory delivery, and opening the door for future sales are important elements of "closing a sale." The better we get at this, the more successful we can be at selling whatever product or service we represent.

When you work from a spiritual perspective, you are sensitive to the needs, interests, and desires of your clients and prospects. It helps to care what makes them hurt, to notice what makes their eyes light up, and what gives them confidence in you.

We, here in North America, have been so blessed that many of the things we describe as "needs" are considered luxuries elsewhere on the planet. Yet all of us tend to think of desires and needs as being the same. Whether we make a distinction or not, we follow the same buying response path to satisfaction. All you need to do is to watch a few of the fantastic sales tools we call television commercials. The deodorant and mouthwash companies avoid talking about eliminating odors—they sell us "confidence!" Tire companies sell us safety, not rubber wheels. Vitamin companies sell us health, vitality, and energy, not pills. Makeup companies sell us beauty, youth, and sexual attraction, not makeup. As Charles Revson, founder of Revlon Cosmetics said, "In the factory we make cosmetics; in the store we sell hope."

You get the idea, don't you? Selling is based on the premise that we enable our clients to fulfill their wishes by purchasing our products and services. Real estate salespeople don't sell houses, they sell homes; they don't sell buildings or land, they sell investments and security. In short, don't sell *things*. Sell ideas, feelings, happiness, and whatever the prospect wishes and desires!

Therefore, conscious selling is helping people discover what they want, and how to get it. Frank Bettger, whom Dale Carnegie called the best salesman he'd ever met, said that the greatest principle in successful selling is this: "When you show a man what he wants, he will move heaven and earth to get it." From beginning to end, the whole process of sales is one of invitation and response. It is more akin to romance, negotiation, and persuasion than it is to pressure, outwitting, and warfare.

Some sales systems are built upon an adversarial relationship with the prospect. There are even some schools of thought founded on the idea that business is war. The idea seems to be that the prospect has some of our money, and we've got to take it back by force, guile, or intimidation. Such approaches may prove effective with a limited number of people, for a limited time, but they are not the tactics that can deliver a successful and enjoyable career. Most of all, these tactics are not spiritual in nature. They go against our soul's calling. Frankly, I believe these tactics are destructive to the well-being of our society as a whole. Personally, my goal is to be in harmony with myself and anyone I am sharing my time and life with at work.

The ultimate goal of this book is to remind you that your powers to co-create an incredible sales career are valid and working for you the moment you activate these powers in your life. You do not have to force your life. True success is about attraction. It's about making yourself the kind of person you would want to do business with. If you want honesty, effectiveness, knowledge, and dependability in the people in your life, you have to cultivate those things in your own personality and thinking patterns. Live the Golden Rule and you will find that life returns exactly what you give to it.

Expand into Your Full Potential with a Professional Coach

Face reality—no one gets to the top of their field alone. Everyone needs wisdom and advice from others who are already successful in the sales field. A professional coach can be a powerful asset to your career by offering you feedback, setting accountability, and providing inspiration and resources that you might not find on your own. What would your career look like if you . . .

- Established professional and personal goals?
- Identified and learned to build on your strengths, talents, and experience?
- Identified your personal blind spots and obstacles and ways to overcome them?
- Developed effective time management skills?
- Developed effective and usable stress management skills?
- Developed your problem-solving and decision-making abilities?
- Tapped into your potential and improved your performance?
- Overcame anxieties and fears about your future?
- Created habits that improve your productivity?
- Successfully brought closure and completion to existing projects?
- Implemented new projects and created action plans?
- Learned to adapt and capitalize on change to use it to your advantage?
- Created balance and harmony between your personal and professional life?

Within each of us lies a massive amount of potential. We all have dreams and desire to live the good life. But how do we do that? Just wanting to be successful doesn't ensure that we can find the way to achieve our dreams alone. Success experts say human beings only use five to 15 percent of our natural potential. That means we have at least 85 percent more potential within ourselves to manifest the life and financial security that we want.

Most people talk about what they want but only a small number of people actually take any action on making their dreams a reality. The truth of life is that if you don't take action you will not achieve exactly what you want. To be able to utilize that extra 85 percent of your potential, you need a mentor or a coach to accelerate your progress, to provide focus and awareness of how to use your life energy. As Woodrow Wilson said, "I not only use all the brains I have, but all the brains I can borrow."

Remember, how you spend your life energy (mental, physical, emotional, spiritual, and financial) determines what outcomes you get in life. To change your life you must use your life energy in an effective and efficient manner. You must actively invest in yourself and your future with wise information that helps you move to the next level in your career and life.

You must understand the value of information if you really want to make a difference in the world and be successful. There is an old joke about the poorest people in North America having the largest television sets and the richest people having the biggest libraries. The caliber of information that goes into your mind will determine the caliber of income you will achieve as a salesperson. You must seek out experts who can provide the right caliber of information to you.

The purpose of a coaching program is to assist you to transform the *quality* of your life in all areas. A good coach can help you improve your professional performance, enhance the quality of your personal life, and build a solid foundation for success. From that foundation your greatest potential for learning, achievement, and success can be activated. This is what I call investing in your "intellectual capital." You must raise your investment in your intellectual capital in order to position yourself for success.

Working with a professional coach will help you, as a conscious salesperson, determine where you want to go in the future. It will help you determine how to create intentions, to make choices, and to take actions that will help activate the natural talent and potential within you.

In our society we have become so reactive to the needs of daily life that we often forget to apply our life energy toward our real goals. Being part of a coaching process will give you the opportunity to break free of the daily reactive cycle. You and your coach will use your time together to be sure that you get the support you need to stay in touch with your passion, dreams, hope, and purpose. Together you will work to overcome your fears and doubts and to find the necessary motivation, tools, and resources to keep you taking the right steps, day by day, to reach your goals.

As a mentor and professional success coach, I believe that it's our decisions, not the conditions of our lives, that determine our future and destiny. You must realize that you are responsible for the fulfillment of all your dreams. The power to succeed or fail is always yours to choose. Make the choice today to be a student of success principles and to be a lifelong learner. All top executives and athletes use coaches; so why not you?

Prayer to Be of Service in My Sales Career

Dear God,

Inspire me to honor my customers, to be of service in the most effective and efficient ways possible. Help me to find just the right ways to expand into my full potential as a conscious salesperson. I know that divine love surrounds all the activities of my life, including my career. Thank you for your assistance in attracting the customers who are a match for me and my product, service, and company. And so it is.

Power Tool Number 12— The Power of Joy

When I was a small child living on the farm in Virginia, my great-grandmother used to take me on her lap when I was unhappy and say to me, "Choose to be joyful, because when you are joyful God can send His Angels to guide you and help you with anything you need. When you are unhappy God is still there but you just cannot hear Him so you cannot get the answers you want." I have never forgotten her words of wisdom to an upset child. I have found them to be so true. The more joy and lightheartedness I feel, the more in touch with my God Source I feel, and the more I can listen to the guidance that I am offered. The more guidance I get, the better my response in any situation and the greater service I can offer.

In a way, my grandmother was teaching me that my emotions arise from my thoughts. Somehow she knew that if I focused on being joyful, I could not feel overwhelmed by negative feelings that seemed to have no solutions. She was teaching me that what we focus on expands. When you are consciously looking for joy, you will find it, and it will grow.

You know in your heart that when you are feeling joyful, difficult people or situations do not have a lasting effect on you. You are more resourceful and open to new solutions. You handle stress and rejection much better. Joy turns routine tasks into enjoyable experiences, no matter what you are doing. Having fun is an important tool for a conscious salesperson. Henry Ward Beecher said, "A person without a sense of humor is like a wagon without springs, jolted by every pebble in the road."

Your goal must be to become conscious of the fact that this very moment in time is a precious gift. You can get the most power from any moment if you make up your mind to enjoy it. Appreciate it. Honor it. You are not on this Earth to be unhappy or to waste your time and talents. You must make choices that allow your enthusiasm for life to stay with you.

The great Norman Vincent Peale said, "There is real magic in enthusiasm. It spells the difference between mediocrity and accomplishment." Enthusiasm for your work will assist you in finding solutions where there appear to be none, and enthusiasm for life will help you achieve success where it was thought impossible. Keep this in mind: Information does not move people to action, but emotion does. So, if you want to improve your sales and create better relationships, you have to improve your enthusiasm for what you do and how you do it.

I live on the beach at the mouth of the Chesapeake Bay in Virginia. The view is breathtaking and very healing for me. I bought an oversized rocking chair for my deck and started a ritual of taking the time to enjoy sunset on the water whenever possible. One night as I was enjoying the view, I overheard a bunch of kids at the waterfront. Sound travels around the water and I could hear one child say clearly, "Do you know what I love? I love it when the seagulls fly over the water low then fly straight up in the sky." All the kids giggled. The next voice was a little girl saying, "Do you know what I love? I love it when my mom makes real mashed potatoes." For the next 20 minutes each of these kids took turns talking about what they loved. They tried to outdo each other. I was enjoying overhearing all these young souls expressing joy!

After it got dark, the kids went home and I started hearing adults coming out on their porches and talking. The first conversation I overheard was a man saying, "Do you know what I hate?" Then the entire conversation with these adults was about what they did not like about

135

life. These adults were having a contest on how much they dislike life. To be honest, it was depressing. I was so struck by the difference between the kids and adults. The kids were focused very much in the present moment and looking for the good in their lives, and they were so full of joy. The adults in this situation were only focusing on what they did not like and they were miserable!

Today is the day to give yourself permission to take a step back and see the big picture. The past is a locked door; the future will depend on what you do today.

Salespeople tend to take themselves very seriously. Sometimes they get stuck in old attitudes, perceptions, and selling habits. But when you stubbornly hold on to old ideas of the way things should be, you shut yourself off from new solutions, new markets, and new products. Conscious salespeople are more spontaneous and can laugh at their own mistakes. They see the brighter side of life. They know how to have fun and turn routine tasks into enjoyable experiences. That's using the Power of Joy.

We have no real power over the external world, but we do have power over how it affects us. Cultivating a sense of humor and a sense of joy can protect you from the negative attitudes and actions of others. Sir Francis Bacon said, "Imagination was given to man to compensate for what he is not, and a sense of humor to console him for what he is." A good sense of humor can keep you sane in difficult times; it keeps you balanced, gives you a sense of perspective, and can get you gracefully through many situations in which you would otherwise want to tear your hair out.

Remember your point of power is always this very moment in time. As a conscious salesperson, you must honor yourself and become aware of how you spend your life energy. You have 1,440 minutes a day to be conscious that each and every minute of your day is a precious gift. The more you fill your life with joy, the more lighthearted you are, and the more enthusiastically you do everything you have to do, the more you are contributing to life.

You can choose to look at your career in sales as one of adventure and fun. You can wake up in the morning looking forward to the day.

Make a conscious choice that you are going to enjoy what you do and how you do it. It's important to reconnect with your funny button and allow the child within you to come out and play.

Being a conscious salesperson means that you must learn to be flexible, to see the humor whenever possible, and allow yourself to be human. Flexibility makes it possible to respond to change by adapting to varying conditions. Flexibility allows for growth and excitement. Being flexible will allow you to see new opportunities and capitalize on them. When you stubbornly hold on to old ideas of the way things should be, you shut yourself off from new solutions, new markets, and new products.

Take to heart the very old but true saying: Life is a journey, not a destination. Being in sales is a career; but it is not your entire life. The saying, "This is not a dress rehearsal," is also very true. One of the most important assets in the sales field is a sense of humor. We need to stop taking ourselves so seriously. It's very easy to get caught up in reacting to life and not see how serious you have become.

One of the questions I always ask in my seminars is, "How many of you have let an old person move into your body?" People always laugh, but there is truth in the answer to that question. Have you gotten stuck in your attitudes, perceptions, and life habits? Have you allowed yourself to be older than your years?

Think of life as an adventure and enjoy the moment. Look for the lighter side of every situation and don't hesitate to laugh at yourself. Every time you laugh you increase your body's production of endorphins. Endorphins are the "feel good" hormones which imitate morphine in the body. Research suggests that laughter can, in fact, help improve resistance to pain and disease. Laughter can clearly help people feel better.

Choosing to see the humor in your life nurtures your creative side. This creative, positive side of yourself enables you to see new opportunities and to keep your spirits high in times of trial.

It is said that a well-developed sense of humor is one of the most charismatic qualities of a good salesperson. Great salespeople are self-accepting, spontaneous, and laugh at their own mistakes. They see the lighter side of life. They know how to have fun and turn routine tasks into enjoyable experiences. Nurture and value these qualities in yourself because they are very attractive to your clients!

"Laughter is the shortest distance between two people," stated Victor Borge. When you are in sales and you can make your prospects laugh, they relax and feel more in harmony with you. A trust level has been set up. Humor is one of the most important tools in your spiritual toolbox because it can diffuse anger and hostility, conquer pretense, and subdue inflated egos.

As I mentioned earlier, your emotions arise from your thoughts. To stop taking yourself so seriously, it's important to create an internal environment that supports you. Let's face it, there will be a lot of things you cannot change and the better your sense of humor, the better you're going to feel about yourself and your sales career. Humor keeps us sane and gives us a sense of balance. Remember how as a child you loved the absurdity of life. Children do things for the sheer joy of it—they don't care about what others think. They do things simply to have fun. When you choose to have an attitude of joy, you will find fun everywhere.

Don't worry if you feel your sense of humor has diminished over time. You can learn to see and to use humor with a little practice, patience, and a willingness to let the lighter side of life shine through. Begin the process of lightening up with these Creating Joy assignments.

Creating Joy

1. Learn to tell funny stories and jokes. It's just like playing sports; the more you practice it the better you will become. If you have not thought of yourself as funny in the past, begin by reminding yourself daily to notice and appreciate more humor in your life and work. People love to laugh and it's important for your success that you look for the humor in life. People really do say and do crazy things, and real life stories are the funniest to share!

2. Make a commitment to yourself to go out and play more often;

maybe go to a comedy club or an entertaining play or movie. Everyone needs to let go of their troubles for a short time and just relax and laugh. One of the greatest benefits of laughter is that it enables you to gain a new perspective on your problems.

3. Give yourself permission to watch some funny television shows and movies to lighten your mood. Life is serious enough without compounding it by watching drama, soaps, and the news.

4. We become like the people with whom we associate daily. Pay attention to who is upbeat, supportive, and positive in your life and choose to be with them as often as possible. The people who are funny, optimistic, and enjoy life will help you stay in a joyful state.

5. Look for the good news. What you focus on expands. Don't let the daily grind of the news deflate your optimistic attitude. Do not dwell on the negative news on television, radio, or newspapers. Create balance in your life; learn what you need to know but do not focus on what you cannot control.

6. Look for funny cartoons and keep a funny file. Many great salespeople I know send funny cartoons to clients and keep them around the office for humor.

7. Start an e-mail joke list. One of my suppliers called me a few months ago and asked me if I wanted to be put on his list. At least once a week, he sends me a collection of very funny jokes. It's an effective and unique way to advertise to me. Next time I need something that he supplies, am I going to think of him? You bet! (*Important:* Make sure all jokes and cartoons are politically correct. Using humor to slander anyone is not a spiritual approach and may hurt you forever in a client's mind.)

8. Create a new label for yourself. Learn to think of yourself as a flexible person. Give yourself permission—and lots of reminders—to rule your own mind no matter what the outside world throws at you. Commit

to being a more flexible person for the next 21 days and notice how much more productive and creative you can become. When you choose to do things differently, you give yourself the opportunity to see life and your career from a totally different perspective. You become more conscious of how your thoughts form your actions, which form your habits, and how these habits shape your future.

Framing Your Focus

Most of us go through life making work tougher than it needs to be. Without realizing it, we have programmed ourselves not to enjoy our present moments. We ambush our minds with negative, self-defeating messages like, "This job is too hard, and I wish I didn't have to deal with these people. I'm not good at this."

Behavior experts say that about 80 percent of our thoughts are negative. These negative, self-defeating thoughts literally program our mental computer to overlook the joy in our lives. Why are we doing this to ourselves? It's hard to feel motivated to make a sale or start new projects when you've already decided that these things are going to be difficult.

Stop programming yourself to believe that work is difficult. Look around at your company's sales staff. It's clear that the salespeople who love their work and have fun are the most productive, the most liked, and the highest paid. So, why not have more fun? Why not enjoy the present moment?

The good news is that you can program your brain to have fun doing something before you do it. Start paying attention to how you make your life and your job harder than they need to be. Since what we focus on increases, choose to focus on creating a life where you're lighthearted, have fun, and feel creative and relaxed. When you allow yourself to have fun, and not take yourself so seriously, your performance usually improves because you are not so tense and stressed out. When you are not tense about your sales career, the clients will line up to buy from you!

The Conscious Salesperson Game

I would like to give you a game to play. In all my workshops I teach this game to help you bring out your natural brilliance and have more adventure and fun in the sales world. It's called the Conscious Salesperson Game. Playing this game, you will adopt a new perspective, a different state of mind. Remember the old saying, "Act the part and you shall become it!"

Take a new approach to your career. Instead of seeing yourself doing what you have always done, dare to envision yourself as someone else who is a master at what they do. Think of someone you admire as a role model for this game. Then simply create a mindset that you are acting as that person.

Do what every child on Earth does: Pretend you are someone who has super powers—in the sales world. You are a good communicator; you love people; you are intuitive, organized, a great time-manager, charming, enthusiastic, knowledgeable, and most of all thrilled to be a salesperson. Everyone responds to you with positive energy.

For three weeks, wake up in the morning and *be* this talented person; do what she would do. Act and talk like this conscious salesperson would. Be confident; act as if nothing in the world can best you. Act as if you are the person you really want to be: a well respected and prosperous superstar in your field. Use your imagination to fully create this new mindset of a wise and respected person. Imagine all the people who look to you as an example of how to act in your field.

As you take on this mindset, you will release your fears and doubts. You will give better presentations because you have sold yourself on you. You will be more efficient. Your skills will improve and, as you focus on envisioning the benefits of happy customers, you will start to actually feel more successful and powerful. Keep in mind that it is possible for you to move past old limitations and frustrations and tap into that God-driven person you want to be. The more you act like what you want to become, the more likely you are to achieve it!

I got a letter from a saleswoman from Canada who had used this game to change her attitude and to improve her sales. She had been bored with her job selling new-construction homes and had been only an average salesperson before she tried the game. Within three months she became a top producer in her company. She told me that, once she started playing the game, her view of her profession and her life totally changed for the better. She went on to say:

> I found that as I envisioned and acted on the premise that I was this superstar salesperson, I released my own fears and doubts about my ability to help people find the perfect home. I found I actually was much more efficient in dealing with people. To my surprise clients responded to me with more respect. I started organizing and filing my paperwork with ease, and before I had always hated doing any kind of paperwork. Before each sales appointment I envisioned the benefits I would enjoy after the sale was completed instead of resisting the process with my usual mutterings of how hard it was to be in sales. To my happy surprise, I had more sales in half the time and I enjoyed the creative process. I was relaxed and confident. I released my own ego and allowed myself to be total partners with God. I knew I could be my best when I was feeling good about myself. Now that I have this new strategy, I know I have the power to use my brain and imagination to improve my performance. After this last month of pretending that I was a top salesperson, I became one! I no longer consider sales difficult or unpleasant. I had programmed myself in the past that these work tasks were painful to me. I clearly was not having any fun until I took charge of my own destiny and changed my perception of who and what I could be in life. Lee, I just want to share one more thing. I gave a speech last week and I pretended to be you when I first got started and it gave me a great deal of confidence and I allowed my true fun self to come out in front of the group and they loved me. Thank you for introducing me to playing the Conscious Salesperson Game.
>
> —Claudia Moss, Canada

Release Your Need to Be Perfect All the Time

One source of stress in our lives as salespeople is our own requirement to appear to be perfect to both our clients and our bosses. Practice saying these few phrases until you are completely comfortable with them. Knowing when to use them and how to use them with integrity will free you to be flexible and creative with your sales clients.

I Don't Know

Many times in the sales process we won't say "I don't know" because we're afraid others will think we're incompetent. It's okay not to know everything—no one does. What you might say is, "That is a very good question and since I am not 100 percent sure of the answer, I will find out and get back to you." Then, just be sure you do get back to them with the correct information when you promised. No worries!

I Need Help

Everyone needs help from time to time. No one can be all things to all people. Salespeople with no support system burn out early in the game. Create a support system that can be there for you when you need help. Think about the situations you face in your job and know in advance how you might need assistance and who might be helpful to you. And don't forget to be helpful to others in the process. What goes around, comes around!

It Was My Mistake or I Was Wrong

No one is right all the time. Even conscious salespeople will have the wrong information sometimes. When you're wrong, admit it, because if you don't, someone else will be saying it for you. I recommend that you apologize at once, then take your valuable emotional energy and go right into problem solving. Right away, ask, "What can we do to fix this situation?"

If appropriate, you might try a lighthearted response, acknowledging your mistake and joking about the predicament. When you resort to a gently self-deprecating demeanor and make fun of the situation, you are conveying grace under pressure, confidence, and credibility.

Remember that the ability to laugh at your own error gives you the flexibility to respond appropriately to difficulty and adversity. You will be better able to keep life in perspective.

No

It's hard saying "no" to people because we want them to like us. We end up giving too much of ourselves—or our profit—because we don't want to disappoint anyone. Salespeople often feel that if they say no to a client, they will lose the sale. Setting appropriate boundaries is just as important within your sales career as anywhere else in your life. Everyone—and every sales deal—has to have boundaries.

The position I now take is to be clear about my boundaries and to tell the truth with kindness (because the truth will set you free). In sales, it's more important to be respected than liked.

It's Not My Job to Make Everyone Happy

There is no way on earth you can make everyone happy. You cannot be all things to all people. Your job is to be the best and do the best that you can.

I was presenting a seminar a few years ago called "Visionary Sales Training." We had a no-questions-asked refund policy; anyone could get a full refund of the seminar fee before noon of each day, for any reason. My program manager came up to me at lunch one day and said, "I have now seen everything to be seen in the public seminar business." She had been outside trying to catch up on paperwork and all she could hear from inside the ballroom was the audience just having a ball, laughing and enjoying themselves. On the first break, some of the seminar attendees told her it was the best seminar they had ever attended and they were totally enjoying the day. Out of the blue at 11:00 A.M., an attendee came to the back table and asked for a refund. The program manager said she was totally shocked when the woman blurted out, "I cannot learn anything in there; people are just having way too much fun!" We happily gave her a refund.

Some people live with a belief system that says that anything new they want to learn or to do has to be difficult and taught in a serious manner. I have just the opposite opinion. The more fun you have as you learn or do something, the better your brain will function, and the better your sales, your relationships, and your life will be.

Start Now!

Being in sales can be a fun adventure. Stop putting off enjoying your life. There are no guarantees that we will be here tomorrow! Your attitude and your behavior affect the results you get daily in your sales and in your life. What positive messages can you give yourself to keep yourself feeling good? How can you be a better role model? How can you have more fun and truly enjoy your life instead of just going through the motions?

While you can, tell the people you love that you love them and tell them often. Send flowers, write notes, give candy, do special things for the people you care about. Be nice to yourself. Realize that life is too short to sweat the small stuff. And, let's face it, folks, most stuff we worry about truly is small stuff in the big picture of life. It's never money or material possessions that really make you happy; it's your relationships with yourself and others. It's the quality of time you have in your life. It's your health and vitality to enjoy life that make you happy. True peace of mind and joy come from moments and feelings that count in life, not from material things.

Whatever you have wanted to do in your life but were waiting for the perfect time to do, stop putting it off—*start now!* Whether it's going back to school, starting a family, or enjoying a hobby, stop wasting your precious life and start doing what brings you joy.

Prayer for Joy

Spirit, help me to take myself lightly so that I may play with the angels. I know that I bring the power of joy into my relationships and into each sales adventure. Thank you for reminding me to be "light" on my feet! Amen.

Afterword

Dear Reader,

Congratulations on your commitment to advance your spiritual knowledge, potential, and destiny. You must realize you are a rare advanced soul to read a book about spiritual sales tools. This book's information is certainly not in the mainstream mindset. You have clearly demonstrated an open-minded philosophy of spiritual knowledge. There is an old saying: "When the student is ready the teacher will appear."

I was honored to be able to share this knowledge with the intention that you will profit from my efforts and hard-earned wisdom. I felt that if I shared this information, maybe I could bring some light (God Source energy) to the sales process. I have now passed the baton over to you to use in the real world of business sales and your life. I challenge you to share your light with the world because one person can make a difference and affect many people.

As in every worthy endeavor, writing this book was both a learning and a growing process for me. Writing this book was a real adventure, and you know what adventures are—sometimes wild rides! As a writer, you never feel you are finished; something could have been said better, or perhaps you did not cover everything you wanted to cover. All writers

I know go through these insecurities, testing their courage in the process of creation.

Writing a book is like giving birth. It takes a long time; it's hard, messy, and sometimes painful. The actual researching, writing, and editing of the material required a massive amount of time from my already well-booked lifestyle. I gained a great deal of hard-earned wisdom from the entire creative process of manifesting this book into reality.

I want you to know if I teach it, I walk it. I am not perfect, but I do my best to walk my talk. Just like you, I am a spiritual being in a human form. I make human mistakes—just ask my editors or my family! I make faulty decisions when I am not connected to my God Source. I struggle like anyone else to take the high road when under stress and fatigue. I have to remind myself almost daily to co-create my life with my God Source and not to just depend on the whims of the marketplace and my business sense to see me through. I have to keep reminding myself to be aware of my self-talk and my mental vibrations. I must take care to envision my goals and my life regularly—just like you.

I sincerely hope you will now share this light unto the world so that, one day in the future, society will embrace a more advanced thinking process and link everything with God Source energy. Please remember that what we say and do in the world has vibrational consequences, and if you want to be a light unto the world, you need to be the best role model possible. You never have to convert anyone to your way of thinking or believing. It is not your job to teach the world what to think. You can be a light on earth by simply being the best you can be at whatever you do. Showing the world what works is better than telling the world what works.

As you live your connection to the God Source, others will observe how you accomplish more with less effort, and have more joy and greater prosperity and peace of mind. They will want to know, "What is your secret?" Feel free to tell them, but only if they ask. If they don't ask, they're not ready to hear the answer. And nothing is more annoying than unsolicited advice!

Think of your life as living art. You have the power to create a healthy, happy, and rich life. Your example will assist others to connect with their own inner spiritual knowledge and connection. Do unto others as you would have them do unto you. Follow the Golden Rule of life and life will reward you. Keep in mind that your point of power is right now. Focus your mental, physical, emotional, and spiritual life energy in the direction of what you want to create. You truly do create your own reality with your thoughts, feelings, desires, and actions. When you connect with your God Source, you will manifest miracles in ways you may never have imagined before. Life is an adventure and you get to write your own script. Give yourself permission to go for it—the whole package of success, respect, joy, prosperity, good health, vitality, good relationships, and peace of mind!

I would be honored if you wrote to me about any positive results you experienced because of what you learned from this book. As an author I appreciate knowing whether my writings in some way added light to your life. I sincerely pray that I have given you some new tools to add to your toolbox of wisdom. I hope if our paths cross you'll introduce yourself and share your stories of success.

God Bless You,
Lee Milteer
www.milteer.com

Bibliography

Addington, Jack, and Cornelia Addington. *Your Needs Met.* Marina del Ray, CA: DeVorss and Company, 1999.

Allen, James. *As a Man Thinketh.* Kansas City, MO: Andrews McMeel Pub., 1999.

Allen, Marc. *Visionary Business: An Entrepreneur's Guide to Success.* Novato, CA: New World Library, 1995.

Anderson, Nancy. *Work with Passion: How to Do What You Love for a Living.* Novato, CA: New World Library, 2004.

Brooks, William. *Niche Selling: How to Find Your Customer in a Crowded Market.* Homewood, IL: Business One Irwin, 1992.

Canfield, Jack. *The Success Principles: How to Get from Where You Are to Where You Want to Be.* New York: HarperCollins, 2005.

Chopra, Deepak. *The Seven Spiritual Laws of Success: A Practical Guide to the Fulfillment of Your Dreams.* San Rafael, CA: Amber-Allen, 1994.

Covey, Stephen. *The Seven Habits of Highly Effective People: Restoring the Character Ethic.* New York: Fireside Books, 1990.

Dyer, Wayne. *Dr. Wayne Dyer's 10 Secrets for Success and Inner Peace.* Carlsbad, CA: Hay House, 2001.

Grabhorn, Lynn. *Excuse Me, Your Life Is Waiting: The Astonishing Power of Feelings.* Charlottesville, VA: Hampton Roads, 2000.

Hicks, Esther, and Jerry Hicks. *Ask and It Is Given: Learning to Manifest Your Desires.* Carlsbad, CA: Hay House, 2004.

Holmes, Ernest. *The Science of Mind,* edited and revised by Maude Allison Lathem. New York: R.M. McBride and Company, 1938.

Kennedy, Dan. *NO B.S. Business Success.* Irvine, CA: Entrepreneur Media, 2004.

————. *NO B.S. Time Management for Entrepreneurs.* Irvine, CA: Entrepreneur Media, 2004.

Keyes, Ken. *Handbook to Higher Consciousness.* Berkeley, CA: Living Love Center, 1973.

Maltz, Maxwell. *Psycho-Cybernetics: A New Way to Get More Living Out of Life.* Englewood Cliffs, NJ: Prentice-Hall, 1960.

Maltz, Maxwell, and Dan Kennedy. *The New Psycho-Cybernetics: The Original Science of Self-Improvement and Success That Has Changed the Lives of 30 Million People.* Paramus, NJ: Prentice-Hall, 2002.

Mandino, Og. *Og Mandino's University of Success.* Toronto/New York: Bantam Books, 1982.

Mann, Richard D. *The Light of Consciousness: Explorations in Transpersonal Psychology.* Albany, NY: State University of New York Press, 1984.

Milteer, Lee. *Feel and Grow Rich: How to Inspire Yourself to Get Anything You Want.* Norfolk, VA: Hampton Roads, 1993.

————. *Success Is an Inside Job: The Secrets to Getting Anything You Want.* Charlottesville, VA: Hampton Roads, 1998.

Peck, M. Scott. *The Road Less Traveled: A New Psychology of Love, Traditional Values, and Spiritual Growth.* New York: Simon & Schuster, 2002.

Piver, Susan. *The Hard Questions for an Authentic Life: 100 Essential Questions for Designing Your Life from the Inside Out.* New York: Gotham Books, 2004.

Popcorn, Faith. *The Popcorn Report: Faith Popcorn on the Future of Your Company, Your World, Your Life.* New York: Doubleday, 1991.

Roberts, Jane. *The Nature of Personal Reality: Specific, Practical Techniques for Solving Everyday Problems and Enriching the Life You Know.* San Rafael, CA: New World Library, 1994.

Roman, Sanaya. *Personal Power through Awareness: A Guidebook for Sensitive People.* Tiburon, CA: H.J. Kramer, 1986.

Ruiz, Don Miguel. *The Four Agreements: A Practical Guide to Personal Freedom.* San Rafael, CA: Amber-Allen, 1997.

Sinetar, Marsha. *Do What You Love, the Money Will Follow: Discovering Your Right Livelihood.* New York: Dell Pub., 1989.

Wilde, Stuart. *The Trick to Money Is Having Some!* Carlsbad, CA: Hay House, 1998.

Williamson, Marianne. *A Return to Love: Reflections on the Principles of "A Course in Miracles."* New York: HarperCollins, 1992.

Index

About the Author

 Lee Milteer is the founder of the Millionaire Mindset Coaching Program, which assists people to be more productive and prosperous. Her powerful presentation style has made her one of North America's most highly regarded human potential speakers and productivity coaches for salespeople and businesses. Lee has been speaking professionally throughout North America and Europe. As president of Lee Milteer Inc., Career Development Strategists, she has counseled and trained thousands of professional people.

Her presentations are so effective that such organizations as Walt Disney, AT&T, Xerox, IBM, Ford Motor Company, Federal Express, 3M, Sales & Marketing Executive International, plus hundreds of government agencies and scores of convention and associations meetings, repeatedly retain her. Lee Milteer has shared the platform with many well-known personalities, such as Dan Kennedy, Jack Canfield, Tony Robbins, Zig Ziglar, Dr. Norman Vincent Peale, Stephen Covey, Brian Tracy, Og Mandino, Ted Koppel, Lynn Redgrave, and Marlo Thomas.

Lee has created and hosted educational programs airing on PBS and other cable networks throughout the United States and Canada. Her video seminars are distributed through the Mind Extension Universe (MEU) Network, reaching 350 of the top *Fortune* 500 companies and major universities. She has developed training films for Bell Telephone, the U.S. Navy, Dun & Bradstreet, the U.S. Air Force, and many private companies.

Lee is a recognized, best-selling audio and videotape author whose products have been endorsed by Nightingale Conant, SyberVision, and CareerTrack. She is the author of the books *Feel and Grow Rich* and *Success Is an Inside Job: The Secrets to Getting Anything You Want,* and coauthor of *Reach Your Career Dreams.*

Lee is a regular guest on TV and radio shows, and has appeared as a Human Potential expert on *The Sally Jessy Raphael Show,* CNN's *Sonya Live,* and *The Montel Williams Show.* She has also hosted and produced her own cable television show, *LifeStyles,* and had her own advice segment on Canada's #1 rated daytime talk show, *The Dini Petty Show.* In addition, Lee has been an expert guest on radio shows throughout North America and has been interviewed by numerous magazines, trade journals, and newspapers, including *USA Today.*

With an extensive background in sales and marketing and commercial real estate, Lee was the owner and president of an electronics equipment sales and leasing company. She attained top honors as "Highest Rated Speaker" while with CareerTrack, North America's premier seminar and training company, for whom she has presented public seminars in over 100 cities annually.

In recognition of her many achievements, Lee received an honorary doctorate in Motivational Theory from Commonwealth College. She was awarded the "Rising Star Award" by General Cassette Corporation, named "Most Outstanding Young Woman" by the Jaycees, and "Most Professional Woman in Hampton Roads," and received the Entrepreneurial Woman of the Year award from the National Association of Women Business Owners.

Lee lives in Virginia Beach, Virginia, with her family. For up-to-date information, and information about her coaching programs, go to her website at www.milteer.com. There you will find proven success principles and a holistic approach to assist you in breaking past emotional blocks in order to reach your personal and professional goals.

Lee Milteer's Educational Resources

Audio—CD and Cassette Tape:

Reinventing Your Life: Success Self Programming
Insider Secrets to Success for Entrepreneurs
Overcoming Unproductive Behaviors: How to Break Any Habit
Mastering Leadership Skills
Successful Life Strategies to Capitalize on Change
Twelve Steps to Total Transformation
Take Control of Your Life: Habit Busting Secrets for Women
Secrets of Employee Loyalty and Productivity

- Owner-Manager-Supervisor Kit—Training Programs
- Small Business Employee Effectiveness Kit—Training Programs
- Professionalism: Keys to Performance Excellence and Career Success

Video/DVD:

Coping with Change
Designing Your Destiny

Success Is an Inside Job
Secrets for Looking and Feeling Youthful
Take Control of Your Life

Books:

Success Is an Inside Job
Feel and Grow Rich
Walking with the Wise for Entrepreneurs

For more information or to order, contact us:
www.LeeMilteer.com
Lee Milteer
Millionaire Mindset Coach
Professional Speaker and Author
(757) 460-1818, fax (757) 460-3675
P.O. Box 5653, Virginia Beach, VA 23471

SPECIAL FREE GIFT #1 (*$49.00 value*) **from Lee Milteer**
FREE REPORT:
"How to Set Goals That Bring You Prosperity"
or "Health Is an Inside Job"
by Lee Milteer

To obtain your FREE report simply photocopy this page, complete ALL the information required, and then either
1. Fax this form to (757) 460-3675, or
2. Mail to: Lee Milteer Inc., P.O. Box 5653, Virginia Beach, VA 23471.
Please allow 2 to 3 weeks for delivery by e-mail. Providing information below constitutes permission for Lee Milteer Inc. to contact you with information about its products and services.

Name_____

Business Name_____

Address _____

_____

City/state/zip or postal code _____

Country_____

Phone_____Fax_____

E-mail Address_____

Please print clearly.

Choose report 1 or 2 _____

1. "How to Set Goals That Bring You Prosperity"
2. "Health Is an Inside Job"

SPECIAL FREE GIFT # 2 *($297.00 value)* **from Lee Milteer**

TWO FREE 60-minute tele-seminars

Enjoy two months of the Millionaire Mindset Program with Lee Milteer. Lee's Millionaire Mindset Coaching will inspire, motivate, and educate you on some of the most important tools you need to be successful as a salesperson. Don't miss this opportunity to hear Lee Milteer LIVE on these educational tele-seminars.

To obtain your TWO FREE 60-minute tele-seminars simply photocopy this page, complete ALL the information required, and then either
    1. Fax this form to (757) 460-3675, or
    2. Mail to: Lee Milteer Inc., P.O. 5653, Virginia Beach, VA 23471.

Please allow 2 to 3 weeks for delivery by e-mail. Providing information below constitutes permission for Lee Milteer Inc. to contact you with information about products and services.

Name_____

Business Name_____

Address _____

_____

City/state/zip or postal code _____

Country_____

Phone_____Fax_____

E-mail Address_____

HAMPTON ROADS

PUBLISHING COMPANY, INC.

Thank you for reading *Spiritual Power Tools for Successful Selling.* Hampton Roads is proud to publish an extensive array of books on the topics discussed in this book, topics such as business, sales, motivation, and more. Please take a look at the following selection or visit us anytime on the web: www.hrpub.com.

Megatrends 2010
The Rise of Conscious Capitalism
Patricia Aburdene, best-selling coauthor of *Megatrends 2000*

In *Megatrends 2010*, Aburdene investigates "corporate social responsibility" and identifies seven new megatrends that will redefine business in the coming years.

Hardcover • 248 pages
ISBN 1-57174-456-8 • $24.95

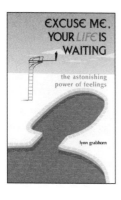

Excuse Me, Your Life Is Waiting
The Astonishing Power of Feelings
Lynn Grabhorn

Ready to get what you want? Get this: hard work and positive thinking can't do it alone. Lynn Grabhorn introduces you to "The Law of Attraction" and uncovers the hidden power of positive feeling. This upbeat yet down-to-earth book reveals how our true feelings work to "magnetize" and create the reality we experience.

Discover the secrets that have made *Excuse Me* a ***New York Times*** bestseller!

Paperback • 320 pages • ISBN 1-57174-381-2 • $16.95
Hardcover • 320 pages • ISBN 1-57174-194-1 • $18.95

Mr. Everit's Secret
What I Learned from the World's Richest Man
Alan H. Cohen, author of *The Dragon Doesn't Live Here Anymore*

Mr. Everit's Secret is a modern-day parable examining our preconceived notions about happiness. When the story's narrator is hired to manage Mr. Everit's wheelbarrow factory, he soon finds he's taken on not only a new job, but also a boss who seems bent on rearranging his entire belief structure. Mr. Everit imparts important lessons about overcoming fear and self-defeating modes of thinking, and taking care of people while letting life take care of you.

Hardcover • 120 pages
ISBN 1-57174-416-9 • $16.95

The Deep Democracy of Open Forums
Practical Steps to Conflict Prevention and Resolution for the Family, Workplace, and World
Arnold Mindell, Ph.D.

Providing practical conflict resolution techniques for groups of 3 to 3,000, *Deep Democracy* is a perfect choice for would-be leaders of family groups, schools, and corporations—anyone wanting to get at the true root of conflict to solve issues for good.

Trade paper • 216 pages
ISBN 1-57174-230-1 • $16.95

Before You Think Another Thought
An Illustrated Guide to Understanding How Your Thoughts and Beliefs Create Your Life
Bruce I. Doyle, III

Doyle's down-to-earth wisdom illuminates a way to change your life. By understanding how thoughts and beliefs affect your experiences, you'll have the key to designing a richer, more fulfilling, life without limits.

Paperback • 128 pages
ISBN 1-57174-076-7 • $11.95

The Invisible Path to Success
Seven Steps to Understanding and Managing the Unseen Forces Shaping Your Life
Robert Scheinfeld

A noted motivational speaker lays out the seven key steps to identifying and working with your inner wisdom and passion to help create the life you want and need.

Paperback • 160 pages
ISBN 1-57174-358-8 • $14.95

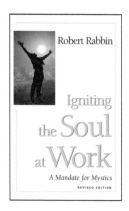

Igniting the Soul at Work
A Mandate for Mystics
Robert Rabbin

A business consultant with spiritual roots shows you how to look beyond the drone of daily work life to find your own true inner vision and bring it to the workplace to transform your life and those around you.

Paperback • 160 pages
ISBN 1-57174-271-9 • $15.95

www.hrpub.com

Hampton Roads Publishing Company

. . . for the evolving human spirit

HAMPTON ROADS PUBLISHING COMPANY publishes books on a variety of subjects, including metaphysics, spirituality, health, visionary fiction, and other related topics.

For a copy of our latest trade catalog, call toll-free, 800-766-8009, or send your name and address to:

HAMPTON ROADS PUBLISHING COMPANY, INC.
1125 STONEY RIDGE ROAD • CHARLOTTESVILLE, VA 22902
e-mail: hrpc@hrpub.com • www.hrpub.com